First World War
and Army of Occupation
War Diary
France, Belgium and Germany

47 DIVISION
142 Infantry Brigade
London Regiment
21st (County of London) Battalion (1st Surrey Rifles)
15 March 1915 - 31 January 1918

WO95/2732/4

The Naval & Military Press Ltd
www.nmarchive.com
Published in association with The National Archives

Published by

The Naval & Military Press Ltd

Unit 10 Ridgewood Industrial Park,

Uckfield, East Sussex,

TN22 5QE England

Tel: +44 (0) 1825 749494

www.naval-military-press.com

www.nmarchive.com

This diary has been reprinted in facsimile from the original. Any imperfections are inevitably reproduced and the quality may fall short of modern type and cartographic standards.

© Crown Copyright
Images reproduced by permission of The National Archives, London, England, 2015.

Contents

Document type	Place/Title	Date From	Date To
Heading	WO95/2732 47 Div Mar 15-Jan 18 1/21 London R.		
Heading	47th Division 142nd Infy Bde 1-21st Bn London Regt Mar 1915-Jan 1918 To 140 Bde.		
Heading	142nd Inf. Bde. 47th Division. Battn disembarked Havre From England 16.3.15. 1/21st London Regt. March 1915 (15.3.15-31.3.15) Jan 18.		
War Diary	Harpenden & S Hampton.	15/03/1915	15/03/1915
War Diary	Le Havre.	16/03/1915	16/03/1915
War Diary	In Train.	17/03/1915	17/03/1915
War Diary	Wizernes.	18/03/1915	18/03/1915
War Diary	St. Hilaire.	19/03/1915	19/03/1915
War Diary	Norrent.	20/03/1915	26/03/1915
War Diary	Oblinghem.	27/03/1915	31/03/1915
Heading	142nd Inf. Bde. 47th Division. 1/21st London Regt. April 1915.		
Miscellaneous	On His Majesty's Service.		
War Diary	Oblinghem	01/04/1915	02/04/1915
War Diary	Les Glaumes.	02/04/1915	10/04/1915
War Diary	Lepugnoy.	11/04/1915	19/04/1915
War Diary	Rue L'Epinette.	20/04/1915	23/04/1915
War Diary	Les Facons.	24/04/1915	24/04/1915
War Diary	Essars.	25/04/1915	27/04/1915
War Diary	Rue L'Epinette.	28/04/1915	30/04/1915
Heading	142nd Inf. Bde. 47th Division. 1/21st London Regt. May 1915.		
Miscellaneous	On His Majesty's Service.		
War Diary	Rue L'Epinette.	01/05/1915	02/05/1915
War Diary	Le Touret.	03/05/1915	04/05/1915
War Diary	Rue L'Epinette.	05/05/1915	07/05/1915
War Diary	Indian Villages	08/05/1915	10/05/1915
War Diary	Le Quesnoy.	11/05/1915	11/05/1915
War Diary	La Beuvriere	12/05/1915	14/05/1915
War Diary	Beuvry.	15/05/1915	15/05/1915
War Diary	Annequin.	16/05/1915	17/05/1915
War Diary	Cuincy.	18/05/1915	20/05/1915
War Diary	Tourbieres	21/05/1915	21/05/1915
War Diary	Bethune.	22/05/1915	25/05/1915
War Diary	Givenchy.	26/05/1915	27/05/1915
War Diary	Beuvry.	28/05/1915	31/05/1915
Heading	142nd Inf. Bde. 47th Division. 1/21st London Regt. June 1915.		
Heading	On His Majesty's Service.		
War Diary		01/06/1915	01/06/1915
War Diary	Verquigneuil	02/06/1915	06/06/1915
War Diary	South Maroc.	07/06/1915	18/06/1915
War Diary	Le Brebis.	19/06/1915	20/06/1915
War Diary	Mazingarbe.	21/06/1915	28/06/1915
War Diary	Philosophe.	29/06/1915	01/07/1915
Heading	142nd Inf. Bde. 47th Division. 1/21st London Regt. July 1915.		

Miscellaneous	On His Majesty's Service.		
War Diary	Philosophe	01/07/1915	04/07/1915
War Diary	Vermelles	05/07/1915	14/07/1915
War Diary	Mazengarbe	15/07/1915	21/07/1915
War Diary	Le Brebis.	22/07/1915	22/07/1915
War Diary	South Maroc.	23/07/1915	31/07/1915
Heading	142nd Inf. Bde. 47th Division. 1/21st London Regt. August 1915.		
Miscellaneous	On His Majesty's Service.		
War Diary	South Maroc.	01/08/1915	03/08/1915
War Diary	Marles Les Mines.	04/08/1915	11/08/1915
War Diary	Houchin.	12/08/1915	18/08/1915
War Diary	Allouagne	19/08/1915	31/08/1915
Heading	142nd Bde. 47th Division. 1/21st London Regiment. September 1915.		
Heading	1/21st London Regt September 1915.		
War Diary	Allouagne	01/09/1915	01/09/1915
War Diary	Haillicourt	02/09/1915	02/09/1915
War Diary	Les Brebis	03/09/1915	03/09/1915
War Diary	S Maroc	03/09/1915	29/09/1915
War Diary	Loos.	29/09/1915	30/09/1915
Heading	142nd Inf. Bde. 47th Division. 1/21st London Regt. October 1915.		
Map	On His Majesty's Service.		
War Diary		01/10/1915	31/10/1915
War Diary	142nd Inf. Bde. 47th Division. 1/21st London Regt. November 1916.		
Miscellaneous	On His Majesty's Service.		
War Diary		01/11/1915	17/11/1915
War Diary	Allouagne	18/11/1915	30/11/1915
Heading	142nd Inf. Bde. 47th Division. 1/21st London Regt. December 1916.		
Miscellaneous	On His Majesty's Service.		
War Diary		01/12/1915	23/12/1915
War Diary	Labourse.	24/12/1915	31/12/1915
Heading	1/21st London Rgt. Jan Vol V.		
War Diary	Vermelles.	01/01/1916	04/01/1916
War Diary	Houchin.	05/01/1916	06/01/1916
War Diary	Bracquemont.	07/01/1916	07/01/1916
War Diary	Trenches	08/01/1916	16/01/1916
War Diary	Bracquemont.	17/01/1916	01/02/1916
War Diary	Trenches.	01/02/1916	05/02/1916
War Diary	Bracquemont.	09/02/1916	11/02/1916
War Diary	Ferfay.	14/02/1916	14/02/1916
War Diary	Allouagne.	16/02/1916	01/03/1916
War Diary	Hersin.	07/03/1916	07/03/1916
War Diary	Hermin.	16/03/1916	16/03/1916
War Diary	Maisnil Bouche.	19/03/1916	30/04/1916
Map			
Heading	1/21 London May 1916.		
War Diary	Villers-Au-Bois.	02/05/1916	25/05/1916
War Diary	Divion.	01/06/1916	01/06/1916
War Diary	Verdrel	13/06/1916	13/06/1916
War Diary	Bully Grenay.	17/06/1916	17/06/1916
War Diary	Sallys.	21/06/1916	21/06/1916
War Diary	Trenches.	25/06/1916	25/06/1916

War Diary	Sains.	30/06/1916	30/06/1916
Operation(al) Order(s)	142nd. Infantry Brigade. Operation Order No. 80.	22/05/1916	22/05/1916
Map	Map Referred To In War Diary For May 1916.		
Miscellaneous	142nd. Infantry Brigade.	22/05/1916	22/05/1916
Miscellaneous			
Heading	142nd Brigade. 47th Division. 1/21st Battalion London Regiment July 1916.		
War Diary	Fosse 10 Sains.	01/07/1916	31/07/1916
Heading	142nd Brigade. 47th Division 1/21st Battalion London Regiment August 1916.		
War Diary	Maizieres.	01/08/1916	02/08/1916
War Diary	Barly.	04/08/1916	04/08/1916
War Diary	St Acheul.	05/08/1916	05/08/1916
War Diary	St Riquier.	05/08/1916	20/08/1916
War Diary	Buigny L'Abbe.	21/08/1916	21/08/1916
War Diary	Vignacourt.	22/08/1916	22/08/1916
War Diary	Villers Bocage.	23/08/1916	23/08/1916
War Diary	La Houssoye.	23/08/1916	10/09/1916
War Diary	Becourt.	11/09/1916	11/09/1916
War Diary	Trenches.	14/09/1916	28/09/1916
Map			
Map	Not To Be Taken Into The Front Line Trenches.		
Map	Map No. 1.		
Map			
Heading	48th Division. 1/5th Gloucester Regt Vol IV 1-30.6.15.		
War Diary	Mametz Wood.	01/10/1916	01/10/1916
War Diary	High Wood.	01/10/1916	07/10/1916
War Diary	Starfish.	08/10/1916	08/10/1916
War Diary	Eaucourt L'Abbaye.	08/10/1916	08/10/1916
Map	Attack By 21st (22nd) Battn 9.0 pm. 8/10/16.		
War Diary	Eaucourt-L'Abbaye.	09/10/1916	09/10/1916
War Diary	Mametz Wood.	09/10/1916	09/10/1916
War Diary	Lavieville.	10/10/1916	15/10/1916
War Diary	Pont Remy.	16/10/1916	16/10/1916
War Diary	Boeschepe	19/10/1916	19/10/1916
War Diary	Vlamertinghe.	19/10/1916	24/10/1916
War Diary	Ypres.	29/10/1916	29/10/1916
War Diary	Railway Dug-Outs (I.20.b).	04/11/1916	04/11/1916
War Diary	Busseboom.	08/11/1916	08/11/1916
War Diary	Woodcote Fm.	18/11/1916	18/11/1916
War Diary	Front Line.	28/11/1916	28/11/1916
War Diary	Ypres.		
War Diary	Front Line.		
War Diary	Busseboom.	08/12/1916	08/12/1916
War Diary	Front Line.	19/12/1916	19/12/1916
War Diary	Reserve.	29/12/1916	08/01/1917
War Diary	Brigade In Reserve.	08/01/1917	08/01/1917
War Diary	Trenches-Canal-Sub-Sector.	18/01/1917	18/01/1917
War Diary	Ypres Salient.	18/01/1917	18/01/1917
War Diary	Divisional Works Battn.	28/01/1917	20/02/1917
War Diary	Trenches Right Section Hill 60. Sub. Sector.	23/02/1917	23/02/1917
War Diary	Brigade In Reserve.	27/02/1917	31/03/1917
War Diary	Moulle.	01/04/1917	07/04/1917
War Diary	Arneke	08/04/1917	11/04/1917
War Diary	Steenvoorde Dickiebush	08/04/1917	11/04/1917
War Diary	Ravine Wood	12/04/1917	12/04/1917

Type	Description	Date From	Date To
War Diary	Halifax Camp.	19/04/1917	19/04/1917
War Diary	Ravine Wood.	27/04/1917	30/04/1917
War Diary	Trenches Left Section Canal-Sub-Sector.	01/05/1917	04/05/1917
War Diary	Halifax Camp.	04/05/1917	04/05/1917
War Diary	Eperlecques	06/05/1917	06/05/1917
War Diary	Connaught And Patricia Lines.	12/05/1917	12/05/1917
War Diary	Left Section-Canal Sub Sector.	13/05/1917	13/05/1917
War Diary	Steenvoorde Area.	20/05/1917	20/05/1917
War Diary	Dominion Lines.	24/05/1917	24/05/1917
War Diary	Left Section Canal Sub Sector.	25/05/1917	25/05/1917
War Diary	Ottawa Camp.	31/05/1917	04/06/1917
War Diary	Woodcote House G.H.Q. 2nd Line.	04/06/1917	07/06/1917
War Diary	Assembly Trenches.	07/06/1917	07/06/1917
War Diary	Second Army Offensive.	07/06/1917	07/06/1917
Map			
War Diary		07/06/1917	10/06/1917
War Diary	28 NW 1/20,000 Might.	09/06/1917	10/06/1917
War Diary	Belgium France 28. Edn.3 1/40,000.	12/06/1917	12/06/1917
War Diary	Caestre.	14/06/1917	14/06/1917
War Diary	Sercus.	15/06/1917	15/06/1917
War Diary	Meteren.	27/06/1917	27/06/1917
War Diary	Ridgewood.	28/06/1917	28/06/1917
War Diary	St Eloi.	29/06/1917	30/06/1917
Map			
Miscellaneous	Message.	11/06/1917	11/06/1917
Heading	Report On Operations Of 21st Bn. On 7th June 1917 London Regt.		
Miscellaneous	142nd Inf. Bde.	10/06/1917	10/06/1917
Miscellaneous	142nd Infantry Brigade.	21/06/1917	21/06/1917
Operation(al) Order(s)	Report Of Operation Of No 5 Platoon B Coy On The Morning Of The 7th June.	11/06/1917	11/06/1917
Map	23rd Divn.-Held Up-Scale 1:5000.		
Miscellaneous	Headquarters, 47th. (London) Division.	14/06/1917	14/06/1917
Operation(al) Order(s)	1/21st London Regt. Report On Part Taken By Battn In Operations Of June 7th-9th Refce Map No 3A. 1:5000.	07/06/1917	07/06/1917
Operation(al) Order(s)	142nd. Infantry Brigade Operation Order No. 186.	07/06/1917	07/06/1917
Map	A Company 21st London.		
Operation(al) Order(s)	Report Of Operations Of No. 6 Platoon "B" Coy On The Morning Of 7th June. 1917.	07/06/1917	07/06/1917
Operation(al) Order(s)	Report Of Operation Of No. 7 Platoon Of B. Coy On The Morning Of June 7.17.	07/06/1917	07/06/1917
Operation(al) Order(s)	Report Of Operations Of No. 7 Platoon "B" Coy 1/21st London Regt On The Morning Of 7 June 1917.	11/06/1917	11/06/1917
Miscellaneous	15 Platoon D Coy of June 1917		
Miscellaneous			
Miscellaneous	A Coy No 193 Platoons.		
Miscellaneous	D Coy F.S.R. Report Of Proceeding During First Stage Of Attack On Z Day.		
Miscellaneous	Report On Operations Of B Coy. 1/21st London Regt On Morning Of June 7th 17.	11/06/1917	11/06/1917
Miscellaneous		11/06/1917	11/06/1917
Miscellaneous			
Miscellaneous	No. 10 Platoon C. Coy (Stoppens Up).		
Miscellaneous			
Miscellaneous	Special Bank-A Position On Our Night Flank.		
Miscellaneous	11 Platoon C. Company.		

Type	Description	Date From	Date To
Miscellaneous	From 2nd Lieut W.H.E. Fransham i/c 2nd Wave Of "A" Coy. (Nos 2 & 4 Platoons).		
Miscellaneous	13 Platoon "D" Coy.	07/06/1917	07/06/1917
Miscellaneous	From O.C.C. Coy The Adjutant Report Of Operations Z Day.	11/06/1917	11/06/1917
Miscellaneous			
Miscellaneous	Report On Movement Of 12 Platoon (Moppers Up.) During Operations 6th June 1917.	06/06/1917	06/06/1917
Miscellaneous	14 Platoon.		
Miscellaneous	Operations By A. Coy. 21st London R.	11/05/1917	11/05/1917
Map	10 Platoon.		
Miscellaneous	Message.		
Miscellaneous		14/07/1917	14/07/1917
Miscellaneous	Headquarters, 47th. (London) Division.	25/06/1917	25/06/1917
Miscellaneous	20 H.Q. 142 Inf Bde.	24/06/1917	24/06/1917
Miscellaneous	From O.C. "C" Coy. To The Adjutant	22/06/1917	22/06/1917
Miscellaneous	Reference G.X. 3/52. 21st June. 1917.	21/06/1917	21/06/1917
Miscellaneous	H.Q. 142 Inf Bde.	13/06/1917	13/06/1917
Operation(al) Order(s)	Operation Order 150.	07/06/1917	07/06/1917
Map			
Map	A Company No. 2 Platoon No. 4 Platoon.		
Map			
War Diary	Refce Maps 28.S.W Sheet. 28 Left Section Right Bde Front S Of Canal.	01/07/1917	01/07/1917
War Diary	Refce Map. Wyschaete 1/10,000.	03/07/1917	08/07/1917
War Diary	Ontario Camp Reninghelst.	08/07/1917	09/07/1917
War Diary	Refce Maps 28 N.W. 1/20,000 28. S.W. Left Section N. Of Canal.	15/07/1917	20/07/1917
War Diary		18/07/1917	18/07/1917
War Diary	Ridgewood Camp.	20/07/1917	20/07/1917
War Diary	Heksken Near Westoutre.	26/07/1917	31/07/1917
War Diary	York Camp Westoutre.	01/08/1917	03/08/1917
War Diary	Ridge Wood Area.	08/08/1917	12/08/1917
War Diary		11/08/1917	11/08/1917
War Diary	York Camp.	12/08/1917	12/08/1917
War Diary	Moringhem.	15/08/1917	22/08/1917
War Diary	Halifax.	23/08/1917	23/08/1917
War Diary	Railway Wood.	24/08/1917	24/08/1917
War Diary	Y Wood.	26/08/1917	26/08/1917
War Diary	Front Line Left Battn Divn Front.	27/08/1917	29/08/1917
War Diary	Cavalry Bks Ypres.	01/08/1917	01/08/1917
War Diary	Menin Road.	01/09/1917	02/09/1917
War Diary	Ypres.	02/09/1917	02/09/1917
War Diary	Dominion Lines H.23.b.	05/09/1917	05/09/1917
War Diary	Steenvoorde	07/09/1917	10/09/1917
War Diary	Ch. Segard. H.30 Central.		
War Diary	Wippenhoek L34.	16/09/1917	16/09/1917
War Diary	Eecke P.17.	18/09/1917	23/09/1917
War Diary	St. Aubin.	23/09/1917	24/09/1917
War Diary	Red Line.	24/09/1917	28/09/1917
War Diary	Red Line.	24/09/1917	01/10/1917
War Diary	Oppy.	02/10/1917	10/10/1917
War Diary	Maroeuil.	10/10/1917	17/10/1917
War Diary	Maroeuil.	13/10/1917	18/10/1917
War Diary	Roundhay Camp.	18/10/1917	25/10/1917
War Diary		19/10/1917	26/10/1917

War Diary	Front Line (Left Of Gavrelle Sector).	26/10/1917	31/10/1917
War Diary	R 2 Sector Front Line.	01/11/1917	05/11/1917
War Diary	Wakefield Camp.	06/11/1917	13/11/1917
War Diary	Oppy.	14/11/1917	19/11/1917
War Diary	Wakefield Camp.	20/11/1917	21/11/1917
War Diary	Mont St. Eloy.	22/11/1917	22/11/1917
War Diary	Berneville.	23/11/1917	24/11/1917
War Diary	Gomiecourt.	25/11/1917	25/11/1917
War Diary	Barastre	26/11/1917	26/11/1917
War Diary	Beaumetz-Les-Cambrai.	27/11/1917	28/11/1917
War Diary	Hindenburg Support Line.	29/11/1917	30/11/1917
Heading	Headquarters 142 Inf. Bde Herewith War Diary For December, 1917.		
War Diary	Hindenburg Support Line.	01/12/1917	01/12/1917
War Diary	Bourlon Wood.	02/12/1917	05/12/1917
War Diary	Hindenburg Support.	05/12/1917	07/12/1917
War Diary	Hindenburg Support Line.	07/12/1917	12/12/1917
War Diary	K.32.a & C.	13/12/1917	15/12/1917
War Diary	Bertincourt.	15/12/1917	16/12/1917
War Diary	Lavieville.	17/12/1917	30/12/1917
War Diary		25/12/1917	30/12/1917
War Diary	Etricourt.	31/12/1917	01/01/1918
War Diary	Lechelle.	02/01/1918	03/01/1918
War Diary	Havrin Court Wood.	04/01/1918	04/01/1918
War Diary	Front Line Ribecourt.	05/01/1918	12/01/1918
War Diary	Lechelle.	13/01/1918	18/01/1918
War Diary	Flesquieres.	19/01/1918	28/01/1918
War Diary	Ypres.	29/01/1918	31/01/1918

WO95/2732

47 Div

Mar '15 - Jan '18

1/21 London R

(5)

47TH DIVISION
142ND INFY BDE

1-21ST BN LONDON REGT
MAR 1915-JAN 1918

TO 140WE

142nd Inf. Bde.
47th Division.

Batt. disembarked
Havre from
England 16.3.15.

WAR DIARY

1/21st LONDON REGT.

MARCH

1 9 1 5

(15.3.15 - 31.3.15)

2/5 Batt⁵ County London Regt.

Army Form C. 2118.

WAR DIARY
INTELLIGENCE SUMMARY.
(Erase heading not required.)

Instructions regarding War Diaries and Intelligence Summaries are contained in F. S. Regs., Part II. and the Staff Manual respectively. Title pages will be prepared in manuscript.

Place	Date	Hour	Summary of Events and Information	Remarks and references to Appendices
Hertford & Southampton	15.3.15		Entrained at HARPENDEN at 1.15 am. – Arrived at SOUTHAMPTON at 6.30 am. – Embarked in SS. MUNICH and sailed at 9 p.m.	A.C.
LE HAVRE	16.3.15		Arrived at LE HAVRE at 5 am. – Disembarked at 7am & marched to No. 6 Rest Camp	A.C.
K. Train	17.3.15		Marched to left Rest Camp at 7.30 am. Entrained. Leaving LE HAVRE No. 4 Dock at 12 noon	A.C.
WIZERNES	18.3.15		Arrived at ARQUES at 7am. – Detrained. Marched to WIZERNES	A.C.
ST. HILAIRE	19.3.15		Left WIZERNES at 8.30 am. & marched via ARQUES & AIRE to ST. HILAIRE	A.C.
NORRENT	20.3.15		Left ST. HILAIRE at 2.30 p.m. for NORRENT	A.C.
"	21.3.15		Church Parade.	A.C.
"	22.3.15		Inspection by the C. in C., British Expeditionary Force. – Night alarm / practice /, 10.30 p.m.	A.C.
"	23.3.15		Company Training. – Digging into entrenching tool. – Attack on trenches.	A.C.
"	24.3.15		Company Training. – Lecon 43rd – Rifles & sight	A.C.
"	25.3.15		Route marches by Companies (half day) – Lectures, notes of – Cleaning, &c.	A.C.
"	26.3.15		Digging. – Route marches	A.C.
" & OBLINGHEM	27.3.15		Moved by Route march. NORRENT – OBLINGHEM	A.C.
OBLINGHEM	28.3.15		Church Parade. Lecture	A.C.
"	29.3.15		Rifles 'A' Coy by the Light Coaley Prince – Bayonet fighting	A.C.
"	30.3.15		Rifles 'B' Coy by the Captain – Coaley Prince – Bayonet fighting – Batting	A.C.
"	31.3.15		Rifles 'C' Coy by the Captain – Coaley Prince – Bayonet fighting – Batting –	A.C.

Moston Turlin W/Col
2/5 London

142nd Inf. Bde.
47th Division.

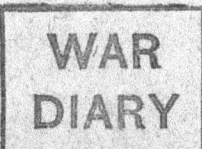

1/21st LONDON REGT.

APRIL

1915

On His Majesty's Service.

WAR DIARY of INTELLIGENCE SUMMARY

Army Form C. 2118.

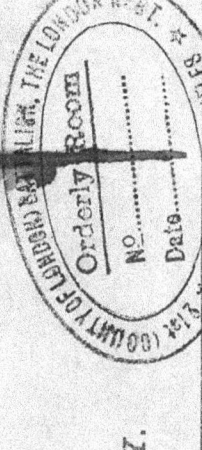

Place	Date	Hour	Summary of Events and Information	Remarks and references to Appendices
OBLINGHEM	1.4.15		(1) Digging by day & by night. Physical Drill & bayonet fighting for remainder	W.C.
LES GLAUNES	2.4.15		hours by route march. The Batt'n. went straight into the Trenches & relieved by 4th Scots Guards Brigade. This was arranged with the Brigade for the issue of cooked rations & the men could have hot mop food that had not been for the kindness of the Batt'n. of the 4th Brigade IT	W.C.
"	3.4.15		In trenches - "A" Coy attached 5th Scots Guard, "B" Coy. to 42nd Highlanders, "C" to 79th Highlanders, "D" to London Scottish	W.C.
"	4.4.15		Do	W.C.
"	5.4.15		Do	W.C.
"	6.4.15		Do	W.C.
"	7.4.15		Do (C. Company N.T.S. & Strathspeys)	W.C.
"	8.4.15		Do	W.C.
"	9.4.15		Do	W.C.
"	10.4.15		Do	W.C.
LERDIGNY	11.4.15		Bn. Returned to LERDIGNY	W.C.
LERDIGNY	12.4.15		Butts & Generally cleaning up after the trenches	W.C.
"	13.4.15		Batt. paraded Bath at BRUAY. Inspection of Transport by G.O.C. 2nd London Division - Inspection of S.A.A. 1st Army	W.C.
"	14.4.15		Physical Drill - Musketry - Company Training (musket exercise, Digging)- Instruction in bombing & range taking	W.C.
"	15.4.15		Physical Drill - Company Training (Musketry Instruction, Construction of Dug-outs) - Instruction in bombing & range taking	W.C.

WAR DIARY or INTELLIGENCE SUMMARY.

Army Form C. 2118.

(Erase heading not required.)

Place	Date	Hour	Summary of Events and Information	Remarks and references to Appendices
LAPUGNOY	16.4.15		Physical Drill - Company Training (Musketry drill, Construction of Gas masks.) Instruction in bombing & map reading	S.G.
"	17.4.15		Physical Drill. Company Training as on 16th	S.G.
"	18.4.15		Church Parade - Musketry Bayonet & Company trainings - Bombing, Sense taking	S.G.
"	19.4.15		Route march to Rue L'Epinette. Took over station of line (2 from 8 p.m.)	S.G.
RUE L'EPINETTE	20.4.15		B+D Companies in front trenches - A+C with Batt. H.Q. in reserve	S.G.
"	21.4.15		As on 20th.	S.G.
"	22.4.15		B+D Companies relieved at 8 p.m. 20th by A+C Companies in the trenches	S.G.
"	23.4.15		Batt. relieved at 8.15 p.m. by 22nd Batt. The Batt. moved billets at LES FACONS	S.G.
LES FACONS	24.4.15		Battn moved 3 Companies to H.Q. L ESSARS. leaving 1 Company at LES FACONS	WD
ESSARS	25.4.15		1 Company moved back to LES FACONS. 200 men as working party (night) at Chocolate Menin.	WD
"	26.4.15		Church Parade -	WD
"	26.4.15		Battalion Parade - 100 men as working party (night) Rue de Bois	WD
"	27.4.15		Relieved 22nd Bn London Regt (D1 art) B Coy Indian Village & C Companies front line	WD
Rue L'Epinette	28.4.15		Trenches	WD
"	29.4.15		Trenches	WD
"	30.4.15		Trenches	WD

142nd Inf. Bde.
47th Division.

WAR DIARY

1/21st LONDON REGT.

M A Y

1915

On His Majesty's Service.

WAR DIARY
INTELLIGENCE SUMMARY.
(Erase heading not required.)

Army Form C. 2118.

Place	Date	Hour	Summary of Events and Information	Remarks and references to Appendices
Rue l'Epinette	1.5.15		Battalion relieved at 8.15 pm by 2/3rd Batt. The Batt. moved to ESSARS and 2 Companies at LES FACONS	
"	2.5.15		Working party of B. 300 men & 6 Officers furnished for INDIAN VILLAGE at 8 pm.	
Le Touret	3.5.15		Battalion relieved 2/3rd Batt. 1 gun M.G. Brigade Reserve with 2 Companies Rue de L'Epinette H.2. 2 Companies at Le Touret. 400 men billeted at BETHUNE	
"	4.5.15		Working party of B. 200 men for htg Village	
Rue l'Epinette	5.5.15		Battalion relieved 2/3rd Battn. at Indian Village HQ, Dn, BG, Dn, AG, L...m., Village. C.G. Reserve Rue l'Epinette	
"	6.5.15		Trenches	
"	7.5.15		Trenches	
Indian Village	8.5.15		Trenches - Transports moved from Rue l'Epinette to INDIAN VILLAGE	
"	9.5.15		Trenches (Heavy bombardment)	
"	10.5.15		Trenches	
Le Quesnoy	11.5.15		Relieved by Bedfords Trenches by Bedfords & billeted at Le Quesnoy	
La Beuvriere	12.5.15		Battalion moved into Billets at LA BEUVRIERE	
"	13.5.15		Battalion bathed at Bruay Fosses	

WAR DIARY
or
INTELLIGENCE SUMMARY.

Army Form C. 2118.

(Erase heading not required.)

Place	Date	Hour	Summary of Events and Information	Remarks and references to Appendices
La Bourriere	14/5/15		Battalion moves to BEUVRY at 6am & bivouacked E on N side of La Bassée	
BEUVRY	15.5.15		Route eventually going into Billets at BEUVRY	
ANNEQUIN	16.5.15		Battalion moves to ANNEQUIN in Brigade Reserve & Billets	
"	17.5.15		Billets at ANNEQUIN in Brigade Reserve	
GUINCHY	18.5.15		Battalion relieves 22nd Battn in trenches at GUINCHY at 11am	
"	19.5.15		Battalion in Trenches	
"	20.5.15		Battn relieved by 22nd Battn. [Neudynthe] C* Coys to Tourbieres A Coy. 6	
Tourbieres	21.5.15		CAMBRIN B Coy into Siding N°1 & Glasgow Road & Willow Lane	
Bethune	22.5.15		Batt relieved & go into Billets at Bethune as Divisional Reserve	
"	23.5.15		Batt billeted at Ecole Nationale	
"	24.5.15		and under O.C. Companies	
"	25.5.15		Batt move to Windy Corner Givenchy- & support 23rd Batt in attack on German trench at 6.30. with H.Q.s at Windy Corner. At 7pm Headquarters removed to Scottish Trench	
Givenchy	26.5.15		4am Headquarters returned back to Windy Corner	

WAR DIARY
or
INTELLIGENCE SUMMARY.

(Erase heading not required.)

Army Form C. 2118.

Instructions regarding War Diaries and Intelligence Summaries are contained in F. S. Regs., Part II. and the Staff Manual respectively. Title pages will be prepared in manuscript.

[Stamp: ORDERLY ROOM, 21st (COUNTY OF LONDON) BATTALION, THE LONDON REGT. FIRST SURREY RIFLES, 1913]

Place	Date	Hour	Summary of Events and Information	Remarks and references to Appendices
Givenchy	27.5.15	3 pm	B att also relieved & men to Billets at BEUVRY	
BEUVRY	28.5.15		Working parties provided for Trenches – Men bathed at Cannes & Refitting	
"	29.5.15	2.0 pm	Men bathed at Bethune Refitting 100 men	
"	30.5.15		" " "	
"	31.5.15		Practice in fitting on masks – Party attends demonstration on Asphyxiating gases	
"			Companies under Company Commanders Refitting	

142nd Inf. Bde.

47th Division.

WAR DIARY

1/21st LONDON REGT.

JUNE

1915

On His Majesty's Service.

21st (County of London) Battalion, The London Regt.
(late Surrey Rifles)
June 1915.

VERGQUIGNEUL	1.6.15	Battalion moved to VERQUIGNEUL at 9.5 pm.
	2.6.15	Platoon training. Battalion Bombers practised.
	3.6.15	"
	4.6.15	"
	5.6.15	"
	6.6.15	Battalion relieves Hertford Battalion in "trenches" W.1 B & D Companies in firing line. C Company in support. A in reserve
South Maroc	7.6.15	Battalion in trenches
	8.6.15	"

WAR DIARY or INTELLIGENCE SUMMARY

Army Form C. 2118.

Place	Date	Hour	Summary of Events and Information	Remarks and references to Appendices
Souchez Maroc	9.6.15		Batt return in trenches	
"	10.6.15		" " "	
"	11.6.15		" " " C. Coy relieves B & A Coy relieves D.	
"	12.6.15		" " "	
"	13.6.15		" " "	
"	14.6.15		" " " B & C Coys in firing line. D. & C. Coys Support & A. Coy Reserve	
"	15.6.15		" " "	
"	16.6.15		" " "	
"	17.6.15		" " "	
"	18.6.15		Battalion relieved in trenches by 10th Battn & move to Le Brebis as Brigade Reserve.	
LE BREBIS	19.6.15		Brigade Reserve. Working party of 158 by night	
"	20.6.15		Battalion moves to MAZINGARBE in Divisional Reserve	
MAZINGARBE	21.6.15		Divisional Reserve. Working party of 200 men by night	
"	22.6.15		" " 100 "	
"	23.6.15		" " 200 "	

WAR DIARY or INTELLIGENCE SUMMARY.

Army Form C. 2118.

Place	Date	Hour	Summary of Events and Information	Remarks and references to Appendices
MAZINGARBE	25.6.15		Divisional Reserve. Working Party of 200 men by night	
	26.6.15		" " " 200 "	
	27.6.15		" " " 200 "	
	28.6.15		Battalion moves to PHILOSOPHE in Brigade Reserve	
Philosophe	29.6.15		Brigade Reserve. Billets close to about 8" Bn London Regt. into PHILOSOPHE	
	30.6.15		" "	
	31.6.15? 1.7.15		Improving Dugouts. Working Party of 175 by night	

142nd Inf. Bde.
47th Division.

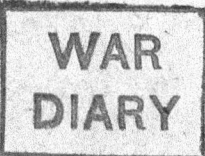

1/21st LONDON REGT.

J U L Y

1 9 1 5

On His Majesty's Service.

Army Form C. 2118.

WAR DIARY
or
INTELLIGENCE SUMMARY.
(Erase heading not required.)

Instructions regarding Diaries and Intelligence Summaries are contained in F. S. Regs., Part II. and the Staff Manual respectively. Title pages will be prepared in manuscript.

Place	Date	Hour	Summary of Events and Information	Remarks and references to Appendices
PHILOSOPHE	1915 Sept 1		In reserve - Digging and Fatigues at night	
	2		Do	
	3		Do	
	4		Do	
Vermelles	5		Frontline trenches ×1 section Headquarters Quality Street	
	6		"	
	7		"	
	8		"	
	9		"	
	10		"	
	11		"	
	12		"	
	13		"	
	14		Battalion relieved moved into billets at MAZENGARBE	
Mazengarbe	15		Digging & Fatigues at night	
	16		Do	

1577 Wt.W10791/1773 500,000 1/15 D. D. & L. A.D.S.S./Forms/C. 2118.

Army Form C. 2118.

WAR DIARY
or
INTELLIGENCE SUMMARY.

(Erase heading not required.)

Instructions regarding ~~Diaries and Intelligence~~ Summaries are contained in F. S. Regs., Part II. and the Staff Manual respectively. Title pages will be prepared in manuscript.

Place	Date	Hour	Summary of Events and Information	Remarks and references to Appendices
	1915			
Mazengarbe	July 16		Digging and fatigues at night	appx
	17		"	appx
	18		"	appx
	19		"	appx
	20		"	appx
	21		"	appx
Le Brebis	22		Moved to Le Brebis in Brigade reserve	appx
South Maroc	23		Took over W1 Section – Headquarters South Maroc	appx
	24		Two Companies in front line. One in support and one in reserve W1	appx
	25		"	appx
	26		"	appx
	27		"	appx
	28		"	appx
	29		"	appx
	30		"	appx
	31		"	appx

142nd Inf. Bde.
47th Division.

WAR DIARY

1/21st LONDON REGT.

AUGUST

1915

On His Majesty's Service.

WAR DIARY
or
INTELLIGENCE SUMMARY.
(Erase heading not required.)

Army Form C. 2118.

Place	Date	Hour	Summary of Events and Information	Remarks and references to Appendices
South Marec	1915 Aug 1		In trenches at N.1	
	2		Division goes into Corps reserve - Battalion relieved & bivouaced near Houchin	
Marles les Mines	3		Move into Billets at Marles les Mines	
	4		Refitting - Drill, Bathing, Instruction and Interior Economy	
	5			
	6			
	7			
	8			
	9			
	10			
	11		Moved into Billets at Houchin	
Houchin	12		Digging on Third Line (SAILLY LABOURSE) 2 companies in morning and two in afternoon.	
	13		" "	
	14		" "	
	15		" "	
	16		" "	

Army Form C. 2118.

WAR DIARY
or
INTELLIGENCE SUMMARY.
(Erase heading not required.)

Instructions regarding War Diaries and Intelligence Summaries are contained in F.S. Regs., Part II. and the Staff Manual respectively. Title pages will be prepared in manuscript.

Place	Date	Hour	Summary of Events and Information	Remarks and references to Appendices
	1915			
HOUCHIN	Aug 17		Digging on third line at Sailly LABOURSE	
	18		Moved to ALLOUAGNE	
ALLouagne	19		Inoculation, Vaccination. Physical and tactical exercises, Musketry, Bathing and Refitting	
	20		"	
	21		"	
	22		"	
	23		"	
	24		"	
	25		"	
	26		"	
	27		"	
	28		"	
	29		"	
	30		"	
	31		"	

142nd Bde.
47th Division.

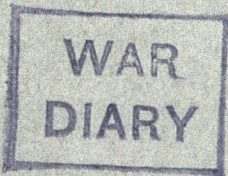

1/21st LONDON REGIMENT.

SEPTEMBER

1916

1/21st London Regt.
September
1915

INTELLIGENCE SUMMARY.

(Erase heading not required.)

Place	Date	Hour	Summary of Events and Information	Remarks and references to Appendices
Allouagne	1915 Sept 1		2 hours march drill - moved to new billets at Huillicourt	
Huillicourt	2		Billets inspected - Batt. paraded preparation of Sergts Hounds Reports &c	
			Batt. paraded by coys - two days & nights digging - returning to billets at Les Ardins	
Les Ardins	3		moved into trenches in W1 South sector	
S Marie	4, 5, 24		} in trenches	
	29		moved into S line trenches at Loos	
Loos	30		moved into advanced trenches in Loos	

Com<u>dg</u> 21st (County of London) Battalion
The London Regiment,
(First Surrey Rifles)

142nd Inf. Bde.
47th Division.

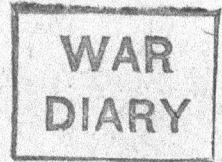

1/21st LONDON REGT.

OCTOBER

1915

On His Majesty's Service.

Army Form C. 2118.

WAR DIARY
or
INTELLIGENCE SUMMARY.
(Erase heading not required.)

Instructions regarding War Diaries and Intelligence Summaries are contained in F.S. Regs., Part II and the Staff Manual respectively. Title pages will be prepared in manuscript.

Place	Date	Hour	Summary of Events and Information	Remarks and references to Appendices
	1915			
	Oct 1		Bn. relieved at 1am by French troops, marched to Houvrac	
	2		marched to Tongueières	
	3		Church Parade	
	4		Route march	
	5		Lecture Ceremony	
	6		Route march to Meaux les Mines	
	7		Route march	
	8		Bn. "Stood-to" all night	
	9		Route march	
	10		Church Parade	
	11		Route march	
	12		Bathing. Bn. garrisons the Philosophe Keeps	
	13		Reserve Trenches	
	14		do Bn. relieves & marches to Mazingarbe	
	15		Brigade Reserve	
	16		do	

1577 Wt.W:10791/1773 500,000 1/15 D. D. & L. A.D.S.S./Forms/C. 2118.

WAR DIARY
or
INTELLIGENCE SUMMARY.

(Erase heading not required.)

Army Form C. 2118.

Instructions regarding War Diaries and Intelligence Summaries are contained in F. S. Regs., Part II. and the Staff Manual respectively. Title pages will be prepared in manuscript.

Place	Date	Hour	Summary of Events and Information	Remarks and references to Appendices
	1915 Oct 17		Bn practises attack on flagged plan of Hulluch	
	18		do	
	19		do	
	20		Bathing	
	21		do	
	22		moved to support trenches sects B2	
	23		In trenches B2	
	24		do	
	25		do	
	26		Bn HQ & one Coy moves back to old German support trench	
	27		moved into front line B2	
	28		In line trenches	
	29		do	
	30		do	
	31		moved back to old German front line and then on to Brigade Reserve	

142nd Inf. Bde.

47th Division.

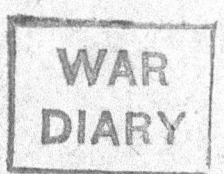

1/21st LONDON REGT.

NOVEMBER

1915

On His Majesty's Service.

WAR DIARY
or
INTELLIGENCE SUMMARY.
(Erase heading not required.)

Army Form C. 2118.

Place	Date	Hour	Summary of Events and Information	Remarks and references to Appendices
Brigade Reserve	Nov 1			
	1915 Nov 2		Relief carried out.	
	3		do	
	4		Our support first reached & sector	
	5		Sent out tenches	
	6		do	
	7		do	
Brigade Reserve	8		Relieved at 9 pm returned to Brigade Reserve at Mazingarbe	
	9		do	
	10		Bathing	
	11		One Coy (B) Fatigues at Redoubt	
	12		Celebration of H.M. Coronation	
	13		Bn moved to Camp Rebeuf at Allouagne Rest March to take Bn into Sam Kitts line of huts	
	14		Church Parade	
	15		Training, Lectures, Economy & Refitting	
	16		do	
	17		do	

Army Form

WAR DIARY
or
INTELLIGENCE SUMMARY.
(Erase heading not required.)

Instructions regarding War Diaries and Intelligence Summaries are contained in F. S. Regs., Part II. and the Staff Manual respectively. Title pages will be prepared in manuscript.

Place	Date	Hour	Summary of Events and Information
Alexandria	1915 Nov 18 to Nov 30		Cairo Barracks. Training, Refitting & Interior Economy

142nd Inf. Bde.
47th Division.

WAR DIARY

1/21st LONDON REGT.

DECEMBER

1915

On His Majesty's Service.

21st (County of London) Battalion. The London Regt.
(1st Surrey Rifles)
December 1915.

Nov 1	Entrained "Rol" to Thieves	
" 2	Returned to Allonagne	
" 3	Training Refitting & Interior Economy	
to Dec 14	do	
" 15	Took over trenches from 12th Royal Scots	2 Coys in front line supports 2 Coys in Reserve billets. Sector of front line D.1. G.3.c. 22nd Bn [Lon Regt] on our left. } front line D.1. G.3.c. 22nd Bn [Lon Regt] on our left 19th Bde on our left. One principal work consists of cleaning mud & laying head gratings
" 16	Companies changed positions	14/1st Bde our own right relieved by 14/1st Bde
" 17	Companies changed positions	
" 18		
" 19	Companies changed positions	
" 20	Companies changed positions	
" 21		
" 22		
" 23	Relieved at 11.30 am by 17th & 18th Lon Regt. Marched by platoons to LABOURSE in Divisional Reserve	

1577 Wt. W10791/1773 500,000 1/15 D. D. & L. A.D.S.S./Forms/C. 2118.

Army Form C. 2118.

WAR DIARY
or
INTELLIGENCE SUMMARY.
(Erase heading not required.)

Instructions regarding War Diaries and Intelligence Summaries are contained in F.S. Regs., Part II. and the Staff Manual respectively. Title pages will be prepared in manuscript.

Place	Date	Hour	Summary of Events and Information	Remarks and references to Appendices
LABOURSE	1915 24th Dec.		Bn in Divisional Reserve at Labourse in billets.	
	25th Dec		Christmas day Parade Service at LABOURSE. Interior economy.	
	26 Dec.			
	27th	6.30	Batt. took over C.2. (fort line - support) from 22nd Bn London Batt. 24th Batt. & Riffle Bde & Riffle Bde.	
	28.		C.2. Coy working & cleaning mud & wate & laying hand gratings.	
	29.	8.00a	Batt. relieved by 22nd London, moved into Brigade Reserve at NOYELLES.	
	30.		" Resting & changing clothes.	
	31.	5.00 p	" moved into support 2 coys in BURLEY TRENCH & 2 coys at VERNELLES.	

[signature]
LT COL.
COMMANDING
21ST LONDON REGT.

WAR DIARY
INTELLIGENCE SUMMARY

Army Form C. 2118.

21st Batt London Regt

Place	Date	Hour	Summary of Events and Information	Remarks and references to Appendices
			Reference / FRANCE 36C 1/40,000 Scale.	
	1916.			
VERMELLES	1st Jan.	4.0am	Took over front line trenches (C.1) G12a.5.5. to G11B.88. from 24th LONDON Regt — 23rd LONDON Regt on left — 4th LANCS Regt on right. — HQ in Old German lines	
	2nd		Own support line shelled heavily from 9.30am onwards. Trench mortars being used as well	
	3rd		Intermittent shelling during the morning, minning [mining] suspected on right flank	
	4th	7.0am	Relieved by 3rd Batt Rumoulid? Brigade, without casualties. Marched to SAILLY and thence & Proton Bunes to HOUCHIN. Battn under Canvas.	
HOUCHIN	5th & 6th		Battn cleaning Kit and equipment and billeting at Minies.	
BRACQUEMONT	7th	3.0pm	marched to BRACQUEMONT and billeted for one night in the CORONS.	
TRENCHES	8th		huston Bunes took Battn to trenches MAROC sector G.4.B. 24th LONDON Regt on our right 140th Bde on left.	
	12th	5.30p	Battn relieved by 24th LONDON Regt and went into Brigade reserve at S. MAROC.	
	14th	6.15pm	Went into trenches on right of last position 22nd LONDON Regt on right. 24th LONDON Regt on left — relieved 23rd LONDON Regt trenches included the foot of Double Crassier and 400 yards of North Arm — minenwerfer used against this position also rifle grenades and bombs.	
	15th	5.30p	Battn relieved and marched into Divisional Reserve at BRACQUEMONT.	

M Huny
Lt. Col.
COMMANDING
21st LONDON REGT

Army Form C. 2118.

WAR DIARY
~~INTELLIGENCE~~ SUMMARY.
(Erase heading not required.)

Instructions regarding War Diaries and Intelligence Summaries are contained in F.S. Regs., Part II. and the Staff Manual respectively. Title pages will be prepared in manuscript.

21st Batt LONDON Regt.

Place	Date	Hour	Summary of Events and Information	Remarks and references to Appendices
			Reference FRANCE 36c. 1/40,000 Scale.	
BRACQUEMONT	1916 17th JAN		Bathing and issue of clean clothing etc in Divisional Reserve	
	18th			
	20th		Batt. marched to trenches in front of LOOS about the COPSE M.G.a. with H.Q. in LOOS	
			23rd Batt: LONDON Regt on right 22nd LONDON Regt on left remained in this position four days	
	23rd			
		9.00 a.m	Our engineers exploded a mine on our right front after we had withdrawn to support trenches. A crater about 60ft in diam with large mouth at sides was formed which was immediately occupied and consolidated near edge — work continued till dawn — work continued on night of 23rd under heavy fire from enemy trench mortars and machine guns.	
	24th	6.30 h	Batt. relieved by 24th LONDON Regt — moved to Brigade Support behind LOOS all our trenches heavily shelled	
	26th	6.0 p	Batt. took up advanced support positions owing to great artillery activity on the part of the enemy. 3 Coys in at disposal of 3rd Bn Batn in front line & remainder at disposal of Brigade.	
	27th		Heavy shelling of our support trenches & billets with shrapnel & H.E. and "tear" shells	
	28th		Heavy shelling continued all day — our artillery very active 9.30 pm Batn relieved by 19th LONDON Regt and marched to DIV Reserve at BRACQUEMONT to remain at one hour notice. Batt. exploits in billets 245a. 29th Jan.	
	29th 30th		Batt. refitting & greatly cleaning — small working parties at MAZINGARBE — 100 men each day.	

[signature] Lt. Col.
COMMANDING
21st LONDON REGt

1577 Wt.W1c791/1773 500,000 1/15 D.D.&L. A.D.S.S./Forms/C. 2118.

Army Form C. 2118.

WAR DIARY

INTELLIGENCE SUMMARY.
(Erase heading not required.)

21st Battn. LONDON RGT.

Instructions regarding War Diaries and Intelligence Summaries are contained in F.S. Regs., Part II. and the Staff Manual respectively. Title pages will be prepared in manuscript.

Place	Date 1916.	Hour	Summary of Events and Information	Remarks and references to Appendices
			Reference FRANCE 36c 40,000 Edition Sheet 5 or HAZEBROUCK. 1/100,000	
BRACQUEMONT	1st Feb	3.0p	Moved to Front line Trenches about M.9.b. to foot of Paille Crassier H.Q. in House in S. MAROC. French Army on right and 24 LONDON RGT on left. Three coys of 9th R.M.F. attached for instruction as in front line.	
TRENCHES	5th Feb	4.30p	Companies changed position, while Battn. R.M.F. attached. Enemy very worrying each night & showed trench & wire immediately in front of our position on patrols report. 6th Feb 9pm enemy working party & artillery opened fire – dispersed them immediately. 6th Feb 9pm children ? field and trench bombard being on our right. Our own trenches in good condition & very little battle fire.	
BRACQUEMONT	9th Feb	8.40p	Battn. relieved by 17th Battn. London Regt. & marched to DIV RESERVE billets.	
	11th Feb		Issue of practice smoke helmets.	
	14th Feb	10.0a	Obtained for Lillers & thence marched to FERFAY to Billets, in Army Reserve.	
FERFAY				
	16th Feb	9.45a	marched to ALLOUAGNE to previous billets, whither Battn. & started leaving 21st R.C.	
ALLOUAGNE	22nd Feb	9.45a	marched as a Brigade to manoeuvre area did up outpost line N of ERNY ST JULIEN. Relieved at ENQUIN - LES-MINES. Battalion & Brigade training which there in snow & low weather.	
	29th Feb	9.30	marched back to billets in ALLOUAGNE in a big ace convoy about 4.15 pm. Remy dismissed en route at AVETTES.	

1577 Wt. W10791/1773 500,000 1/15 D. D. & L. A.D.S.S./Forms/C. 2118.

[signature]
O.C. 21st Battn. London Rgt.

Army Form C. 2118.

WAR DIARY
INTELLIGENCE SUMMARY.
(Erase heading not required.)

21st Batt. LONDON REGT.

Instructions regarding War Diaries and Intelligence Summaries are contained in F.S. Regs., Part II. and the Staff Manual respectively. Title pages will be prepared in manuscript.

Place	Date 1916	Hour	Summary of Events and Information	Remarks and references to Appendices
			Reference. FRANCE 36.b. 10.a.a.p. E.d.b.	
ALLOUAGNE	1st March		Refitting battⁿ with Boots & Clothing — bathing at mine MARIE-LES-MINES. general battalion & company training & route marches — Battⁿ placed at 3 hours notice to entrain at LILLERS	
HERSIN.	14th March		Brigade moved under orders of 2nd DIV. Battⁿ to HERSIN. Digging & general working parties daily & nightly under 2nd DIV. 12th Brand Baths at SAINS-EN-GOHELLE.	
HERMIN	15th March		moved under 47 Div to HERMIN. to billets, training & route marching.	
MAISNIL BOUCHE	19th		to MAISNIL BOUCHE to Hutments in Div Reserve. training	
	21st		moved to VILLERS AU BOIS in support — training & working & carrying Parties.	
	26th	10.0p	relieved 7th London Reg^t in front line trenches about S.2.d. one coy in front line S.2.d. ABLAIN a. one i. inneediate support — cap inter relief each night. front line consisted of "Granne Butts" badly enfiladed. (relieved 1/4/16.)	

R Schmeltyn Lt. Col
COMMANDING
21st LONDON REGT

1577 Wt. W10791/1773 500,000 1/15 D.D.&L. A.D.S.S./Forms/C. 2118.

WAR DIARY
of
INTELLIGENCE SUMMARY.
(Erase heading not required.)

Army Form C. 2118.

Instructions regarding War Diaries and Intelligence Summaries are contained in F. S. Regs., Part II. and the Staff Manual respectively. Title pages will be prepared in manuscript.

Place	Date	Hour	Summary of Events and Information	Remarks and references to Appendices
	1916 APRIL			
	1st	11.0 pm	Relieved in front line trenches about S.W. 2.d. (36c.Map) by 17th London Regt & marched to Billets at VILLERS-AU-BOIS. — Transport & stores in permanent Billets in PETIT SERVINS.	Ref map 36c.
	2nd	noon	Marched to reserve billets at VERDREL. Batt training and working parties of 200 men each day & night — baths & clothing on 4th & 6th for whole Battn.	
	7th	9.45 am	Moved to Billets & Huts at MAISNIL-BOUCHÉ	
	8th	4.30 pm	Moved by Coys to Support in VILLERS AU BOIS. Specialist training & musketry day & night working parties — Church parade 9/4/16	
	13th	7.0 am	Batt changed areas sending two coys and specialists to CARENCY	
	14th	9.0 am	Batt relieved 8th London Regt in A Sub Sector CARENCY Section about M.5. A.14 central. 24th London Regt on left. 46th Div on right. Fairly quiet mining activity on our right — trench mortars & rifle grenades	
	20th	11.0 pm	Relieved in trenches by 18th London Regt and marches back to Billets in reserve at MAISNIL BOUCHÉ. Batt inspected by Maj Gen Comdg 47 DIV. & addressed by GOC 4th Corps. Batt training, musketry and gymnastics.	
	26th	4.0 pm	Moved to VILLERS AU BOIS in support — Carrying parties to Tunnels Coy & Batt training daily — hostile mines exploded on our right flank.	
	30th	7.30 pm	Stand-to — mine exploded on our front — stand down 8.30 h all quiet.	

Manuel Lt Col
Commanding
21ST LONDON [Regt]

— Present British Line
— Present German Line
— Lines to be regained & consolidated
— Lift for Artillery Barrage at moment of Assault

S

Uhlan Alley
Ers⁰ 23/14
Alley.
Landwehr Av
International Avenue
Victoria Avenue
B Central

1/21. London

May 1916

47
Army Form C. 2118.
(42)
Originals

Vol 13

WAR DIARY or INTELLIGENCE SUMMARY.
(Erase heading not required.)

Instructions regarding War Diaries and Intelligence Summaries are contained in F. S. Regs., Part II. and the Staff Manual respectively. Title pages will be prepared in manuscript.

21st Battⁿ London Regt

Place	Date	Hour	Summary of Events and Information	Remarks and references to Appendices
VILLERS-AU-BOIS	1916 MAY 2nd	8.0 pm	Battⁿ marched by Coys to former sector of trenches at S.14.b. in front of SOUCHEZ and on the VIMY RIDGE. — 24th London Regt on our left and XVII Corps (Loyal North Lancs) on our right.	
	3rd	4.47 pm	After extensive Arty work and rapid preparation the 176th Tunnelling Coy exploded four mines in front of our sector — just breaking our front line. — Our artillery fired immediately on German front & support lines and on its lifting at 6.45 pm we occupied the three large craters formed (see attached map). Our covering parties of Lewis Gunners and Bombing Groups held the enemy off, whilst our working parties consolidated the lip near our Y trenches being dug up to the craters and strengthened & improved during the night. At dawn our covering parties withdrew to our left where we commanded the whole of the craters found from the parties dug.	
	4th		The rest was continued during our remainder of time in trenches	
	✠ 8.15	11.0 pm	Relieved by 20th London Regt and marched back to ESTREE CAUCHIE to reserve billets	
	14th	7.0 pm	Marched by coys to relieve 20th London Regt in same sector as before — German artillery noticed to be increasing in volume and much more activity on part of Trench Mortars and snipers.	
	20th	11.0 pm	Relieved by 20th London Regt and marched to ESTREE CAUCHIE to reserve billets	
	21st	6.30 pm	Heavy German bombardment burst and Battⁿ ordered to stand to in billets — sight of our former sector attacked and pushed back (see map).	
		8.35	Battⁿ ordered to march to VILLERS-AU-BOIS and made up to 300 rounds S.A.A. per man (continued)	

WAR DIARY
or
INTELLIGENCE SUMMARY
(Erase heading not required.)

Summary of Events and Information 21st Battn LONDON Regt.

Place	Date	Hour	Summary of Events and Information	Remarks and references to Appendices
(continued)	1916 MAY 22nd	1.30 a.m.	Battn moved from reserve at VILLERS to position in MAISTRE LINE about X.23.d. arriving in position about 3.0 a.m.	
	22nd	8.20 p.m.	Moved via CABARET ROAD to right half of former position on new R&R (see map) taking over from 20th London Regt and preparing to resume attack.	
	23rd	6.25 pm	Battn attacked position taken by the enemy on evening of 21st May (plotted red on map attached) in conjunction with 24th London Regt and 99th Inf. Bde on our right. A.Coy. attacked supported by C. & D. Coys. who each left one Platoon in reserve. B.Coy. held LOVE and MOMBER craters and front line behind them. Batt. Bombers worked along front line from craters and also bombed up GOBRON and ERSATZ. Our Lewis gun occupied position near crater and other advanced with C.& D Coy. We retook the old front line and held it for about 1½ hours after which an all troops on our right had not succeeded in getting forward we were forced to retire. We then held RETRENCHMENT and GOBRON bombers double flanking on far side. They also made a second attempt assisted by the 22nd London Regt Bombers to regain ERSATZ but were driven back to the reserve line. During these operations all trenches were badly flattened on ? holds artillery and it was with great difficulty that our repairs and communications were carried out. During the night 23/24th we consolidated the position assisted by RE & Pioneer Batt. (4th RWF)	
	24th	4.00 am	and held same till relieved by 23rd London Regt when we withdrew to former Billets in ESTREE CAUCHIE	
	25th	9.0 am	Battn marched to Corps Reserve at DIVION - small draft received and training begun on casualties. Our loss about 150 in recent operations including 7 officers missing and 5 wounded.	

31/5/16.

M. Vinne
Lieut Col. Comdg.
21st Battn LONDON

ORIGINAL

Army Form C. 2118.

WAR DIARY
INTELLIGENCE SUMMARY.
(Erase heading not required)

21st Battn London Regt.

Vol 10

Instructions regarding War Diaries and Intelligence Summaries are contained in F.S. Regs, Part II and the Staff Manual respectively. Title pages will be prepared in manuscript.

Place	Date	Hour	Summary of Events and Information	Remarks and references to Appendices
			Reference Sheet FRANCE 36 to 1/40,000	
DIVION	1916 JUNE 12th		Battn in reserve Billets at DIVION training and receiving small drafts - 14 supernumerary officers added to establishment	
VERDREL	13th	10.0 am	Battn marched to Billets in VERDREL in Divisional Reserve - working parties each night	
BULLY GRENAY	17th	7.0 am	Battn marched to BULLY GRENAY in support to 23rd & 24th London Regt. 4 coys in reserve trenches	
SAINS	21st	10.0 am	Went into reserve at FOSSÉ 10. (SAINS) working over carrying parties by night	
trenches	25th	9.0 pm	Took over front line trenches in SOUCHEZ sector in BOIS EN HACHE - 1st Kings Royal Rifles on our right - 1st Hons Battn R.M.D. on our left. Systematic bombardment of enemy's lines by our artillery each day and night. Raid by 142nd Bde on our left on night of 29/6/16.	
SAINS	30th	11.30 pm	relieved by 15th Battn London Regt and marched to reserve billets in FOSSÉ 10. (SAINS)	

[signature] Lt Col.
COMMANDING
21ST LONDON REGT.

SECRET.   Copy No. 3

142nd. INFANTRY BRIGADE.

OPERATION ORDER NO. 20.

22nd. May. 1916.

Reference 1/10,000 Sheet Map Givenchy.

1. (a). The attached tracing shows present position as regards front line. The G.O.C.47th. Division intends to regain and consolidate after dark tonight the lines shown in RED on tracing as far South as CENTRAL AVENUE. 25th. Division is attacking at the same time to the South of CENTRAL AVENUE.
    Troops and Artillery of 2nd. Division have come into our Area to assist. The 99th. Infantry Brigade is under orders of the 47th. Division.

    (b). The 47th Division attack will be carried by 99th Infantry Brigade (Comdr. Lieut.Col.Barker) and 142nd.Infantry Brigade. (Comdr.Brigr.Genl.Lewis).

    (c). The Southern boundary of the area of 142nd.Infantry Brigade is GRANBY AVENUE (inclusive) - LANDWEHR inclusive ERSATZ ALLEY on West Side of ZOUAVE VALLEY - CABARET ROAD inclusive.

    (d). 142nd.Infantry Brigade is taking over from GRANBY AVENUE inclusive to UHLAN ALLEY exclusive with 24th and 21st London Regts (Orders already issued to Units concerned).

    (e). Artillery have kept the area to be assaulted under continuous fire during the day and will lift at the hour fixed for assault to the line shown in GREEN in tracing.

    (f). 141st.Infantry Brigade will hold remainder of CARENCY SECTN.

    (g). 99th.Infantry Brigade will garrison ALHAMBRA & COLISEUM and strong points in BERTHONVAL SECTION.

2.   The attack of the 142nd.Infantry Brigade is sub-divided into Right attack - Lieut.Col.Carr.24th.London Regt.
            24th.London Regt.
            2.Sections 2/3rd.Lon.Fd.Co.R.E.
            ½.Company.4th.R.W.F.
            Lewis Gun Detachment 23rd.London Regt.
            2.Companies 23rd.Lon Regt (for carrying).
    The objective line shown in RED on tracing from GRANBY ALLEY (inclusive) to ERSATZ (inclusive).

        Left attack Lieut.Col.Kennedy 21st.Lon Regt.
            21st.Lon Regt.
            2.Sections 2/3rd.Field Co.R.E.
            ½.Company.4th.R.W.F..
            2.Companies 23rd.Lon Regt (for carrying).
    The objective line shown in RED on tracing from ERSATZ (inclusive) to point near Junction of TRANCHOT with front line.

3. (a). The attack will be over the open and will be launched at 1.30.a.m. 23rd.May.
Dress - Fighting Order,300 rounds S.A.A. per man.
Rations for 23rd inst on man.
Five Sandbags per man will be carried and 10 bombs per bomber.
Sandbags will be issued at CABARET ROUGE.

(b). Battalion Commanders will detail a garrison for the present Front Line in their Subsection which will be held at all costs and improved during the night.

(c). Ground gained will be consolidated at once.

(d). Battalions will be prepared to form defensive flanks should they penetrate further than the attacks on their right or left.

4. 22nd.Lon Regt.will be in Brigade Reserve in the BAJOLLE & MAISTRE LINES in Brigade Area.
Bombers in former line aHeadquarters at POINT.G.

5. 23rd.Lon Regt less Lewis Guns & Bombers (at CABARET ROUGE) will move to CARENCY Headquarters X.17.d.73.on conclusion of carrying work.

6. Light Mortar Batteries with 2 Stokes Mortars and Ammunition will follow 22nd.Lon Regt and will keep a runner at that Battalion Headquarters.

7. M.G.Battery on West Side of ZOUAVE VALLEY will keep enemy's slope of VIMY RIDGE as far as GIVENCHY under indirect fire from moment of assault.
Reserve Section 142nd.M.G.Company will follow 22nd.Lon Regt and keep runners at their Headquarters.

8. C.R.E.is forming a dump of tools,wire,sandbags etc at CABARET ROUGE which can be drawn on. Col.HAWKES 4th.R.W.F. is in charge of R.E.arrangements and holds 100 men permanent working party in reserve

9. ERSATZ ALLEY will be for <u>IN</u> Traffic only.
130th.ALLEY for <u>OUT</u> Traffic only.
LANDWEHR for traffic both ways.

10. Brigade will be in position for attack by 12.30.a.m. on 23rd.May.

11. Advanced Brigade Headquarters at CARENCY Brigade Headquarters CABARET ROUGE from 11.p.m. 22nd.May.

MAP REFERRED TO IN WAR DIARY FOR MAY 1916
Traced from Aeroplane Photograph.
(not to Scale)

The Crows Nest is a very high Mound of Chalk and Clay thrown up by the Explosion and commanding the surrounding country — a trench was cut to the top of it and this made an excellent observation post — it was however marked by the enemy and could easily have been destroyed by Artillery if used too obviously

POINT X was another high point — it was here that Major HP Richards was killed on the night of 18th May by a German Sniper.

THE VIMY RIDGE

1. The 3 Craters named were occupied by the 21st Battn on evening of 3rd May when the Battn was holding this sector from A. — B.

2. The sector held by the Battn on night of 23rd May is shewn in red lines & captured positions in dotted red.

3. The Southern Boundary was in each case ERSATZ.

WO Kennedy Lt Col
Comdg.
21st Battn London Regt.

SECRET.

142nd. INFANTRY BRIGADE.

Dispositions night 22/23rd.May.1916.

Brigade Headquarters VILLERS AU BOIS.

24th.Lon Regt. Front Line system GRANBY to ERSATZ inclusive Old Headquarters 15th.Lon Regt Headquarters.

21st.Lon Regt. Front Line system ERSATZ exclusive to UHLAN exclusive. Shares Headquarters A Subsection CARENCY.SECTOR.

22nd.Lon Regt. MAISTRE & BAJOLLE LINES. Headquarters POINT G.

23rd.Lon Regt. CARENCY Headquarters X.17.d.73.

142/1 & 142/2.L.M.B's.Reserve Section 142nd.M.G.Company VILLERS AU BOIS.

Reserve Section 141st.M.G.Company. MAISTRE LINE.

J.R. Hunt
Major.
Brigade Major,
142nd.Infantry Brigade.

B.M.939.
22/5/16.

Copies to :-
1. 21st.Lon Regt.
2. 22nd.Lon Regt.
3. 23rd.Lon Regt.
4. 24th.Lon Regt.
5. 142/1.L.M.B.
6. 142/2.L.M.B.
7. 141st.Inf Bde.
8. 99th.Inf Bde.
9. 141st.M.G.Co.
10. 142nd.M.G.Co.
11. 47th.Div.
12. C.R.E.47th.Div.
13. War Diary.
14. File.

H R Hunt
Major,
Brigade Major,
142nd. Infantry Brigade.

Issued to Signals at 9.30.p.m.

Copy No. 1. War Diary.
2. File.
3. 21st. Lon Regt.
4. 22nd. Lon Regt.
5. 23rd. Lon Regt.
6. 24th. Lon Regt.
7. 142nd. M.G.Co.
8. 142/1.L.M.B.
9. 142/2.L.M.B.
10. B.B.O.
11. B.T.O.
12. 141st. Inf Bde.
13. 99th. Inf Bde.
14. C.R.A.
15. C.R.E.
16. 47th. Division.
17. 2/3rd. Fd Co.R.E.
18. Left Group.R.A.
19. 4th.R.W.F.

142nd Brigade.
47th Division.

1/21st BATTALION

LONDON REGIMENT

JULY 1916

WAR DIARY
or
INTELLIGENCE SUMMARY

Army Form C. 2118.

(Erase heading not required.)

21st Batt: London Regt.   Vol XI

Place	Date	Hour	Summary of Events and Information	Remarks and references to Appendices
Fosse 10 & Sains	1916 JULY 1st	2.30pm	Batt arrived in Div Reserve Billets at FOSSE 10 (SAINS) resting and refitting	
	3rd	7.0pm	Moved into Brigade Reserve 300yds N's Bully Grenay remainder at FOSSE 10.	
	9th	4.0pm	Batt relieved 23rd London Regt in front line trenches in ANGRES Section in front of Bully Grenay with 1 Coy R.N. Div attached for instruction 24th London Regt on our Right and the Left Batt on our right - Patrolling - cleaning trenches.	
	14th	4.0pm	Relieved by HOWE Battn RND and marched to Billets in FOSSE ⚊ & Hersin	
	16th	8.0pm	Left HERSIN and relieved 19th Middlesex Regt in support to CARENCY Sector CAMPY	
		11.0(?)pm	(up) HQ and 1Coy at CARENCY, 1Coy at VILLERS au BOIS. Men Coys formed in new trenches	
	24th	11.0pm	Relieved 23rd Battn in night sub-section CARENCY Sector (an old position of 24th Divn)	
	28th	11.30am	Relieved by composite Battn of 20th, 21st, 22nd & 23rd Northumberland Fusiliers & marched back to former billets at MAISNIL-BOUCHE.	
	15th	3.0pm	Marched & Brigade to RAINS (en route for south) arriving and billeting at 5.45 pm	
	30th	5.15am	Batt route march - Batt to MAZIERES Billeted at 9.0 am. Cleaning	
	31st		Cleaning and resting	

[signature]
LT. COL.
COMMANDING
21ST LONDON REGT.

142nd Brigade.
47th Division

1/21st BATTALION

LONDON REGIMENT

AUGUST 1 9 1 6

WAR DIARY
or
INTELLIGENCE SUMMARY.
(Erase heading not required.)

Army Form C. 2118.

1/21 London Regt
Pt 12

Place	Date	Hour	Summary of Events and Information	Remarks and references to Appendices
	1916 August			Reference to maps: Scale 1/100000 Sheet
MAIZIERES.	1st		Batt. Bathing in morning at BERLENCOURT, training in afternoon new Bivouacs smoke helmet drill & musketry.	LENS 11.
	2nd	6.15 pm	Batt. marched in Brigade to billets in BARLY (16 miles) arriving at 1.0 am 3/8/16. – one day's rest and bathing in river in afternoon	
BARLY.	4th	4.10 am	Batt. marched out of BARLY and marched in Brigade to ST ACHEUL (7 miles) arriving at 7.30 am	ABBEVILLE 14.
ST ACHEUL	5th	4.40 am	" " " " " " ST RIQUIER (11 miles) " " 11.0 am	
ST RIQUIER.			A fortnight's training at ST RIQUIER on IV Army training ground – digging and attacking trenches – route marches – bathing in river.	
BUIGNY L'ABBÉ	20th	10 pm	Batt. left and marched in Brigade to BUIGNY L'ABBÉ (4 miles) arriving at 4.0 pm in billets for a night	LENS 11.
VIGNACOURT.	21st	4.0 am	" " " " VIGNACOURT (16 miles) " " 2.30 pm	
	22nd	1.0 am	" " " " VILLERS BOCAGE (7 miles) " " 10.30 am	AMIENS 17.
VILLERS BOCAGE	23rd	9.0 am	" " " " LAHOUSSOYE (10 miles) " " 2.0 pm in III Corps area	
LAHOUSSOYE	23rd to 31st		Batt. training and digging 2 days & night – special training of specialist sections and lectures. – Reconnoitering parties of Officers visited scenes of recent fighting East of ALBERT in view of taking over new line.	

M Murray Lt. Col.
COMMANDING
21ST LONDON REGT.

Army Form C. 2118.

WAR DIARY
or
INTELLIGENCE SUMMARY.

(Erase heading not required.)

1/21st LONDON REGT

Instructions regarding War Diaries and Intelligence Summaries are contained in F. S. Regs. Part II. and the Staff Manual respectively. Title pages will be prepared in manuscript.

Place	Date	Hour	Summary of Events and Information	Remarks and references to Appendices
	1916. September		Page I	Reference Maps Europe Sheet
LAHOUSSOYE.	1st		Batt. in Billets training in neighbourhood, practising night work. Artillery formation - attack practice - and digging.	AMIENS. 17.
	10th	8.00am	Batt. paraded and marched to Becourt (via ALBERT) C.O. and Coy Commanders reconnoitring own position and new HIGH WOOD (BOIS DES FOUREAUX).	SHEET 11.
BECOURT.	11th	6.15am	Batt. moved by platoon and relieved Brigade of 1st Division in trenches in and east of HIGH WOOD. which we held for four days under heavy artillery fire - digging + repairing trenches and forming up with trenches recently gained as our right flank	LENS.
Trenches	14th	6.30pm	Batt. relieved by the whole of 140th Infy Bde which occupied assault position previous to an attack intended but to tomorrow + old trenches ½ mile N.E. of FRICOURT.	
	15th	6.30am	Batt. moved + bivouacked in S.E. corner of BOIS de MAMETZ 140th + 141st Bdes attacked at 6.10am.	
		Noon	Batt. was placed at disposal of B.G.C. 140 Bde. - A gap having occurred between 140th and 141st Bdes and the former having failed to reach its final objective. 1B Batth. is ordered to advance from behind HIGH WOOD and to attack for the Eastern corner of same in a half Battn. attached	See map.
		4.45pm	Batth. advanced in Artillery formation to its attack with a fighting strength of 19 Officers and 550 O.R. Arrangements could not be made for Artillery support to cooperate covering fire use on the leading	

Maurice Quill Lt Col Cmdg
21st London Regt

1577 Wt.W10791/1773 500,000 1/15 D.D.&L. A.D.S.S./Forms/C. 2118.

WAR DIARY
or
INTELLIGENCE SUMMARY.
(Erase heading not required.)

Army Form C. 2118.

Place	Date	Hour	Summary of Events and Information	Remarks and references to Appendices
	1916. Sept. (continued)		Page 2.	
			platoons came under observation &, were subjected to intense artillery bombardment and later to heavy rifle and machine gun fire. The casualties in this advance amounted to 14 officers and 490 other ranks of whom a large percentage must have been killed by heavy shells. The remaining 2 officers and a few N.C.O's. me dug themselves in and held on to what ground they had occupy until the Battn. was ordered to withdraw at 7.30 a.m. 16th.	
	16th	7.30 a.m	Battn. withdrew and bivouacked at S.E. corner of BOIS de MAMETZ. under orders of 142 Bde. remaining men of the 4 Coys. were employed as a burial and carrying party at BAZENTIN-le-GRAND.— HQ. of Battn. and waggon lines remained in MAMETZ Wood until Bde. was relieved on 18th.	
	19th	5.0 p	Battn. moved to bivouac at BLACKWOOD ½ mile east of ALBERT	
	20th	2.30	Battn. marched to MILLENCOURT and billeted in the village	
	21st		Draft of 25 men received for 3rd Battn.	
	23rd		Draft of 253 other ranks received of 2/5 East Surrey Regt. & 1st Battn. Serious training and digging began in Indiana cap/vicinity	
	25th	10 pm	Battn. left MILLENCOURT (a/ Div taking over the line) and marched to East corner of MAMETZ wood in Bivouac awaiting orders to move & receiving its attack.	

[signature] Lt Col Comdg 9th Devon Regt

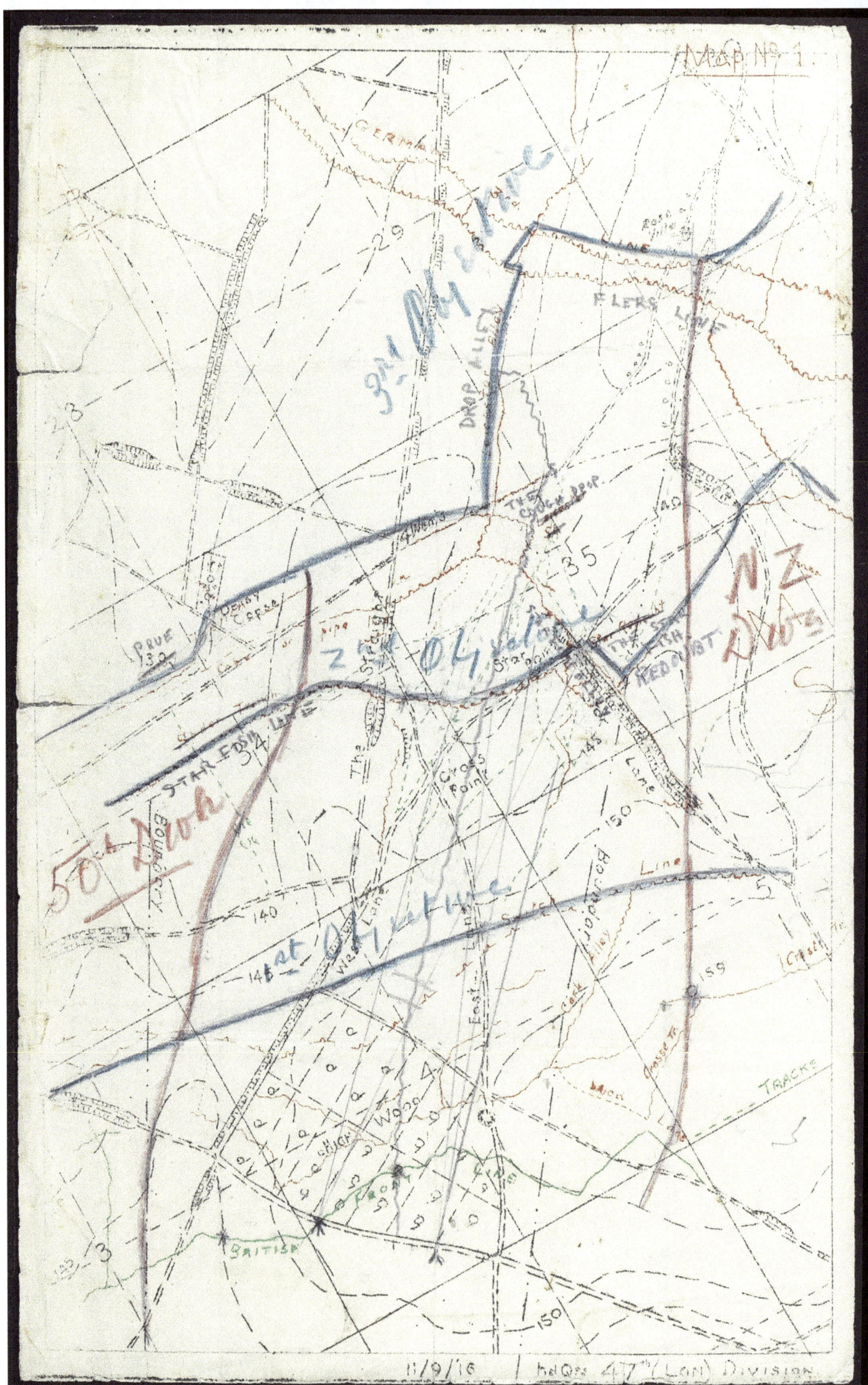

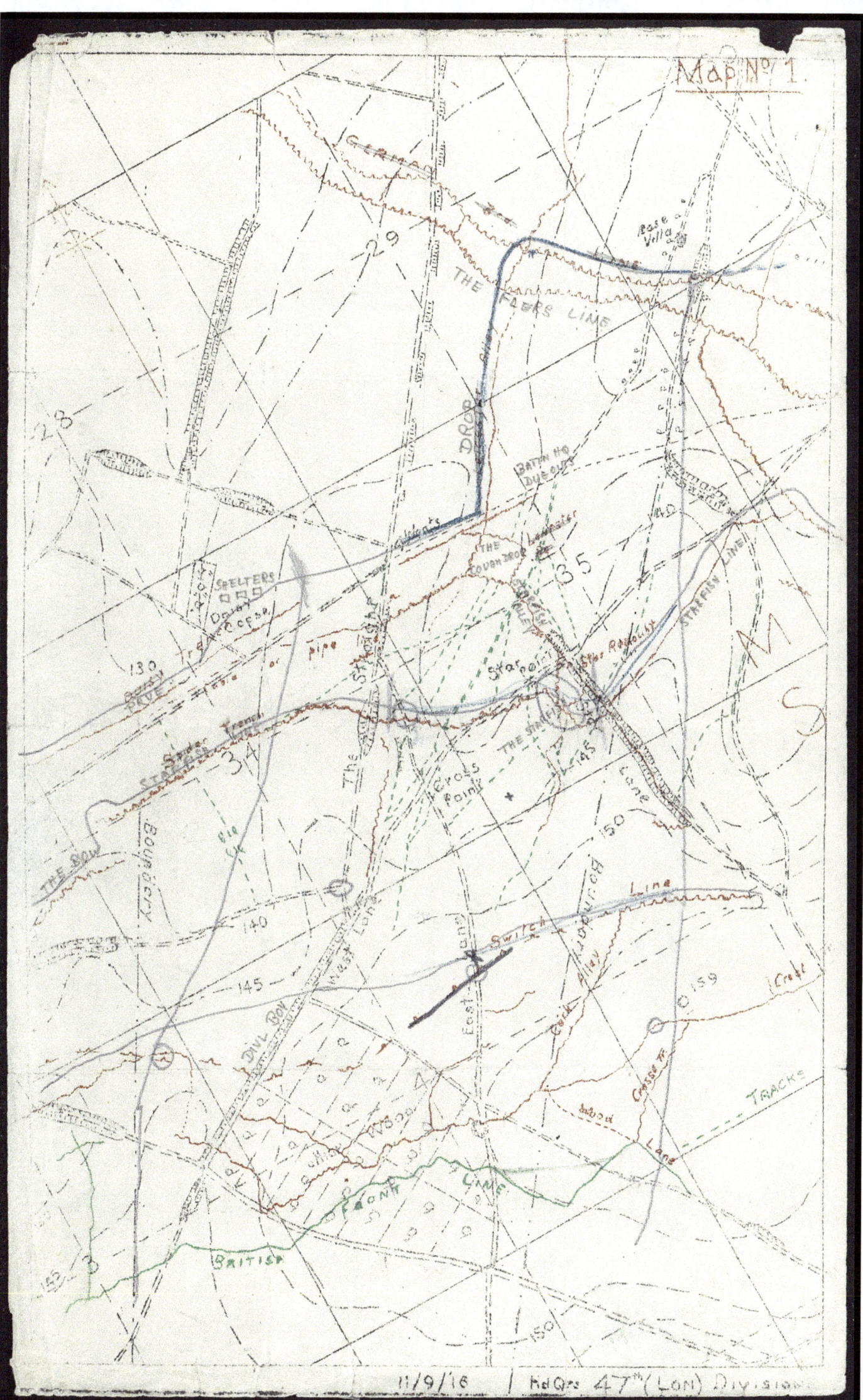

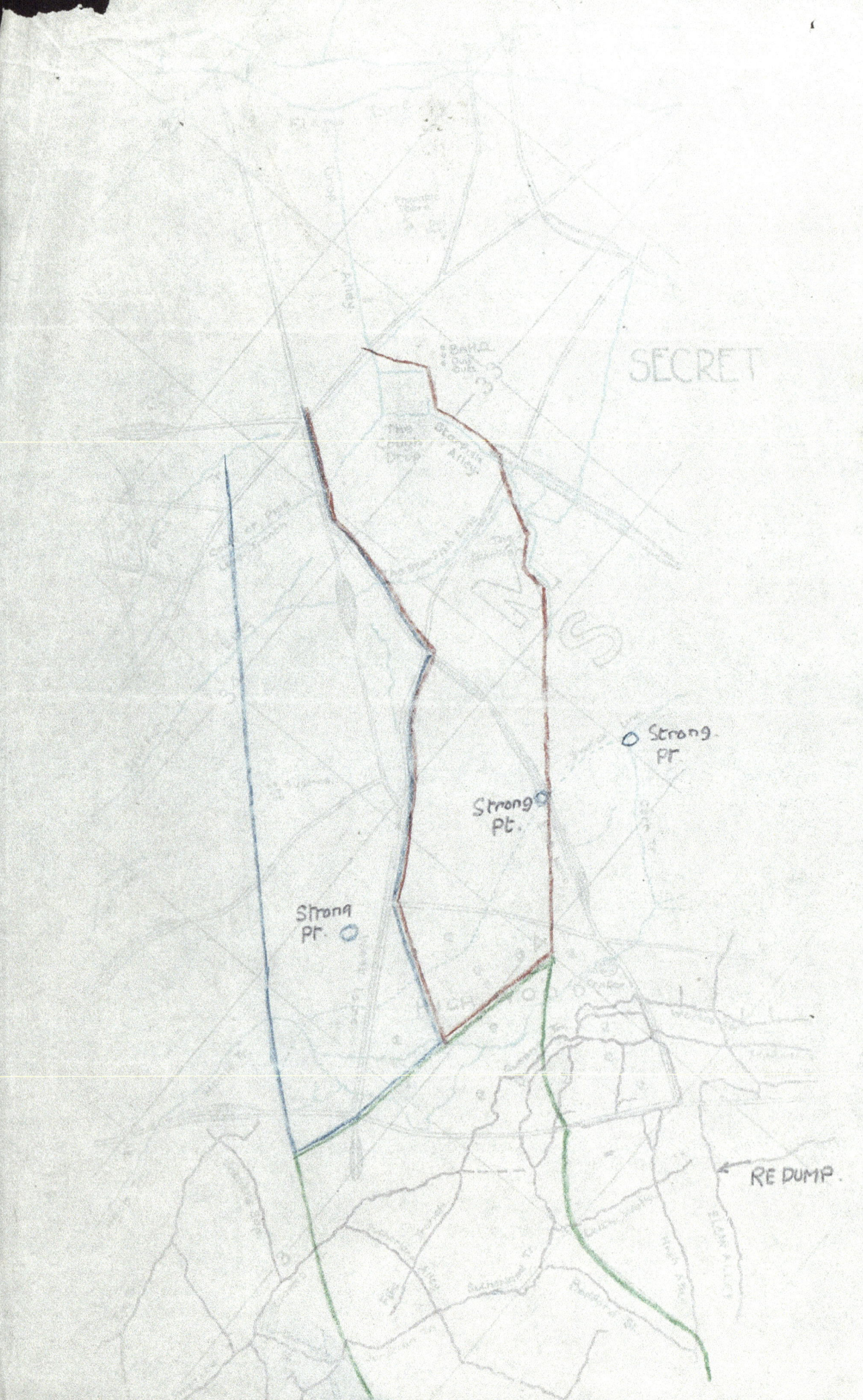

B.M.   H.P.
10 sheets

131/5914

48th Division

115th Knack Regt. 1 — 30.6.15.
V.R.IV.

WAR DIARY
INTELLIGENCE SUMMARY.

Army Form C. 2118.

1/21st LONDON REGT

Place	Date	Hour	Summary of Events and Information	Remarks and references to Appendices
	1916. October		PAGE. I.	Reference map.
MAMETZ WOOD	1st		Battn bivouacked in Brigade in support – necessary fighting stores issued and Battn moved up in fighting order to east side of HIGH WOOD (S.4.d.) to support the attack of 141st Bde on EAUCOURT L'ABBAYE.	Combined Sheet ALBERT 1/40,000
HIGH WOOD	1st 2.0 pm		Battn arrived in position (S.4.d) and remained as carrying and working parties	
	7th 11.0 pm		Battn moved into support trenches round STARFISH REDOUBT (M.35.c.) to replace 22nd LONDON Regt moved forward.	
STARFISH	8th 7.0 am		Battn assumed the position – and received orders to attack at 9.0 pm in conjunction with 22nd LONDON Regt. (see attached map) Attack to be in nature of a surprise without any artillery preparation – conference at noon and scheme explained to officers. maps issued.	see attached map
	4.30 pm		Battn moved into jumping off positions in front of EAUCOURT L'ABBAYE (M.23.b.) facing N.W. with 22nd Battn on left and 140th Bde on right. ZERO to be 9.0 pm.	
	5.0 pm		Orders received altering nature of attack and specifying an artillery bombardment – one minute before Zero insuring a lifting.	
EAUCOURT L'ABBAYE	9.30 pm		Line advanced without any casualties until within 200 yds of enemy trench when the Germans – alarmed by our artillery – turned on intense rifle and machine gun fire which completely stopped our advance. Remnants of Battn attempted to dig in & formed a strong outpost manned by Bombers & Lewis Gunners.	

549

COMMANDING
1/21st LONDON REGT

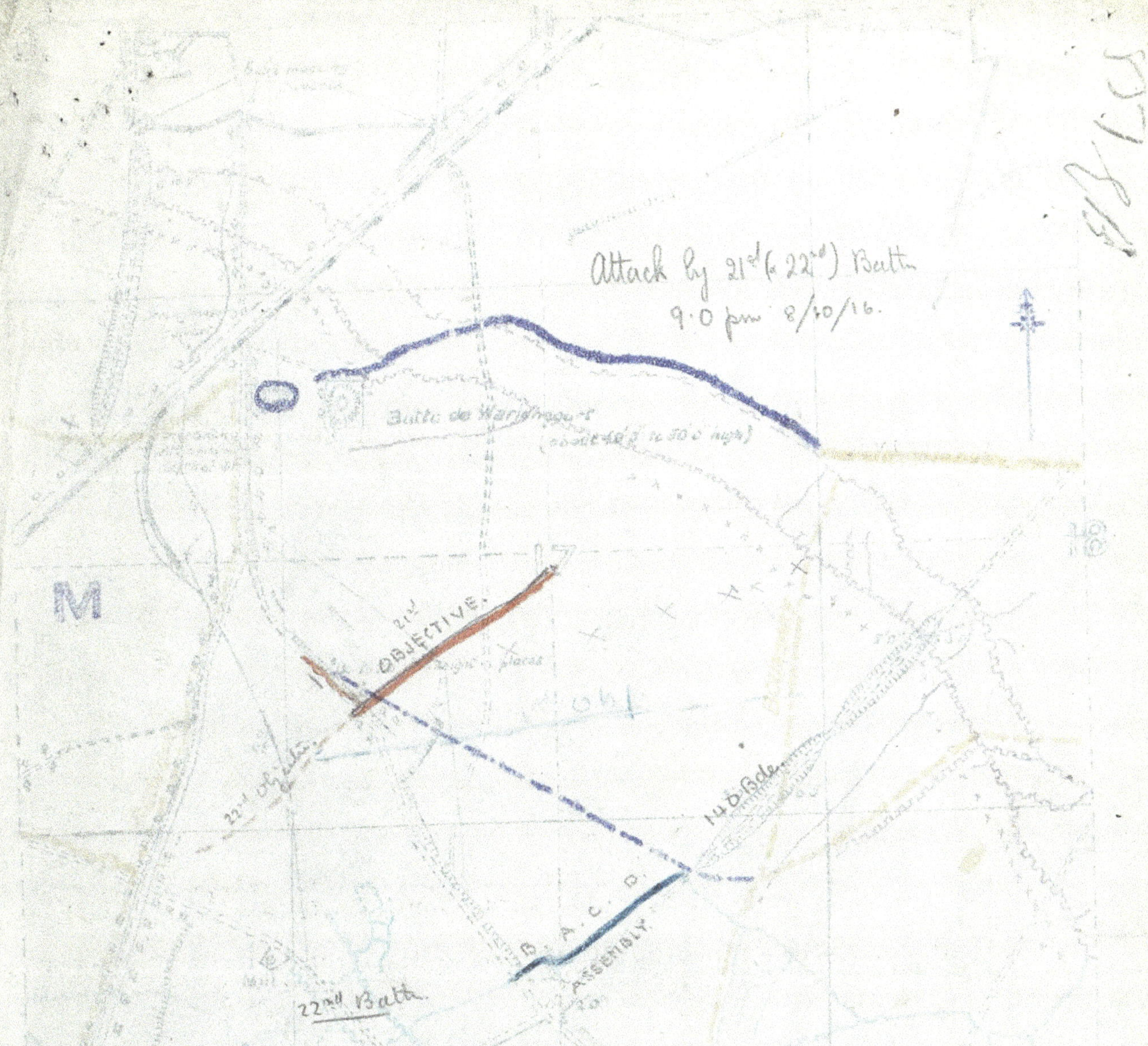
Attack by 21st (& 22nd) Battn
9.0 pm 8/10/16.
O
Butte de Warlencourt
M
21st OBJECTIVE.
22nd Objective
140 Bde.
B. A. C. D.
ASSEMBLY.
22nd Battn
Eaucourt Abbaye
23
24
18
Battn H.Q.

Scale 1:10000.

MAP No 5.

Army Form C. 2118.

WAR DIARY of OCTOBER
INTELLIGENCE SUMMARY.
(Erase heading not required.)

1/21st LONDON REGT.

Instructions regarding War Diaries and Intelligence Summaries are contained in F. S. Regs., Part II. and the Staff Manual respectively. Title pages will be prepared in manuscript.

PAGE II.

Place	Date 1916 October	Hour	Summary of Events and Information	Remarks and references to Appendices REF. MAP
EAUCOURT – L'ABBAYE	9th	2.0 am	2 Coys 23rd LONDON Regt moved up to front line – Battn withdrawing and reorganising in FLERS LINE behind EAUCOURT L'ABBAYE (M.23.c.)	ALBERT & area combined sheet
MAMETZ WOOD.	10th	11.0 pm	Battn relieved by Battn of 1st South African Bde and returned to Bivouac in MAMETZ WOOD.	
LAVIEVILLE	13th	3.0 pm	Battn relieved by 2nd K.O.S.B. and marched back to billets in LAVIEVILLE resting and refitting	
	14th	1.0 pm	Transport moved by road to PONT REMY via AMIENS & resting one night at ST SAUVEUR.	
	15th	12.0 noon	Battn marched to Station ALBERT and entrained for PONT REMY	
		6.0 pm	Battn detrained at LONGPRE – LES – CORPS – SAINTS & marched to Billets at PONT REMY.	
PONT REMY	18th	9.0 am	Battn entrained – proceeded via ABBEVILLE – CALAIS – BOULOGNE – HAZEBROUCK. to GODEWAERSWELDE HAZEBROUCK. 5a. – thence marched to camp a mile north of BOESCHEPE. – reconnoitre line on 18th	Sheet 27 × 28 1/40.00. 1
BOESCHEPE	19th	8.30 pm	Battn bivouacked at CONNAUGHT CAMP – Refitting and resting	
VLAMERTINGHE.	22nd	12.15 pm	Battn marched to HALIFAX Camp in Div Reserve Training and refitting. (H.14.c)	Sheet. 28. N.W.
	24th	4.0 pm	Battn moved into Bde Reserve at BELGIAN CHATEAU 1½ miles SW of YPRES. (H.23.b.)	
YPRES.	29th	5.0 pm	Battn moved into support at RAILWAY DUGOUTS (I.20.b) Working Parties etc. 2 Coys in close support in strong points just behind front line. (proposed stay for 5 days.)	

[signature]
Colonel
COMMANDING
1/21st LONDON REGT

Army Form C. 2118.

WAR DIARY
or
INTELLIGENCE SUMMARY.
(Erase heading not required.)

Summary of Events and Information 1/21st LONDON REGT.

Place	Date	Hour	Reference Map. Belgium Sheet 28 N.W.	Remarks and references to Appendices
YPRES. Railway Dug-out (I.20.b)	1916 Nov. 4th	7.0 pm	Moved to front line trenches I.29.c.5.0. to I.29.d.9.9. Holding line and carrying out works. 141st Inf Bde on our right and 23rd Div on left.	
BUSSEBOOM	8th	11.0 pm	Battn relieved by 6th Battn London Regt & returned to Rest at Scottish Camp (G.23.a) Training. Bathing - refitting and cleaning lines. (By train from YPRES to BRANDHOEK	
WOODCOTE FM.	18th		Brigade moved into the line (BLUFF SECTOR) Battn to reserve at WOODCOTE FM (I.20.c.) supplying carrying parties and work.	
front line.	28th	5.0 p	Battn relieved 22nd Battn in front line from I.34.b.4.0. to I.34.b.9.6. much work in progress to the winter. Enemy quiet on this front - very little artillery. 2nd Battn London Regt on our right and 141st Bde on left	

Ohalford. Major Condy
1/21st London Regt.

Vol/76

Army Form C. 2118.

WAR DIARY
or
INTELLIGENCE SUMMARY.
(Erase heading not required.)

1/21st London Regt

Place	Date	Hour	Summary of Events and Information	Remarks and references to Appendices
	DEC. 1916		Ref map. BELGIUM 28. N.W.	
YPRES. Front Line	8th		Bluff Sector. I.34.b.4.0. to I.34.b.6.9.6. Battn Holding line 23rd Battn on right 1/4th Bde on Left.	
BUSSEBOOM.	8th	9.30p	Battn relieved by 8th London Regt and marched into Reserve at Scottish Camp BUSSEBOOM (G.23 a) remained in reserve training new men - specialists - bathing - and refitting - weather very wet.	
Front line	19th	4.0p	Battn relieved 1/8 London Regt in Hill 60 Sector (right) from I.34.b.9.8. to I.29.c.5.1. 8th Battn on our right 23rd Battn on our left. a great deal of work necessary on the defences. - weather very bad. - Christmas Day in the front line passed very quietly. Germans were heard singing on Christmas eve otherwise no indication of the season.	
Reserve	29th	6.30p	Battn relieved by 22nd London Regt & marched to HALIFAX CAMP. (H.14.C.) and supplied working parties in front & new line daily. - Battn celebrated Christmas day in the usual way with dinners & concert on 31st Dec. Lt Col H B Kennedy D.S.O. took temporary command of 142 Infty Bde on 26/12/16	

Arthur Patterson
Major
Comdg. 1/21 London Regt.

Army Form C. 2118.

WAR DIARY
INTELLIGENCE SUMMARY.
(Erase heading not required.)

1/21st Battn London Regt.

Vol 17

Place	Date	Hour	Summary of Events and Information	Remarks and references to Appendices
Reserve	1917 Jany. 1 – 8		Battn in Huts at HALIFAX CAMP (H.14.c.) providing working parties for left Brigade area day and night. – weather wet and windy.	
Bug Now – Camp	8	3pm	Battn moved to the Huts at SCOTTISH LINES (G.23.a.) and trained under Brigade Training Scheme. Bayonet dummy work, musketry, smoke helmet drill, bayonet fighting, and musketry, was the chief feature of the training which was greatly interfered with owing to the inclement weather and lack of space for training.	
TRENCHES – CANAL SUB SECTOR YPRES SALIENT	18	10 pm	Took over front line trenches – LEFT SECTION – CANAL SUB-SECTOR from 18th LONDON REGT – 24th London being on our right and 8th LONDON REGT being on our left. Owing to anticipated trouble from the enemy on January 27th, Kaiser's Birthday, our artillery systematically bombarded enemy lines day and night, to which little retaliation was received on our own lines. 20th LONDON relieved 8th LONDON on our left on night of 26th Jany, and 23rd LONDON relieved 24th Battn on our right on following night. Little enemy activity was experienced on 27th Jany. During the whole period weather was very cold – there being 2 hard frost all the time.	
DIVISIONAL WORKS BATTN.	28	10 pm	Relieved by 22nd Battn LONDON REGT and marched to Huts at DICKIEBUSH (H.27.6.) Battn under Canadian Battn made DIVISIONAL WORKS BATTN and in consequence furnished large working parties area).	
	29 – 31		returning later men for specialist training	

Burkitt Lt. Col
COMMANDING
1/21st LONDON REGT

WAR DIARY
INTELLIGENCE SUMMARY

Army Form C. 2118.

Vol 18
1/21ST LONDON REGIMENT.

Place	Date	Hour	Summary of Events and Information	Remarks and references to Appendices
			Ref MAP BELGIUM 28 N.W.	
DIVISIONAL WORKS BATTN.	1917 FEBY. 1-3		Batln in Huts at DICKIE BUSH [H.27 b.] Large working parties away, and time devoted to the training of Specialists.	
	5 –	2pm	Batln moved to the Huts at SCOTTISH CAMP [G 23 a.] and devoted time as above.	
			About 500 men were allotted away at various camps in the vicinity, and for the most part were employed on light Railways. Occasional daily parties were supplied for unloading ammunition at AHEELE and drawing R.E. without casualties was ended, in the form of carrying parties, for the proposed raid which was successfully carried out by 6th Bn on 20th inst.	
	20 –	9 pm	Batln moved from SCOTTISH CAMP to HALIFAX CAMP on night of 20th and reassembled on 23rd having been relieved by 15th LONDON REGT as DIVISIONAL WORKS BN.	
TRENCHES Right Section Hut 60. Sea Secret	23	8pm	Took over front line system from 22nd LONDON REGT – 23rd LONDON on LEFT and 18th LONDON on our RIGHT. Much work was put in on drainage and salvage, and as a result considerable improvement was recorded on trenches which were shortly withdrawing from recent shell of hard frosts.	
BRIGADE IN RESERVE	27	11pm	Relieved by 8th LONDON REGT, and proceeded to SCOTTISH LINES, using roadway from H 26 a S.W. to BRANDHOEK [G 12 a.] arriving between 2am & 4am	
	28		Devoted to cleaning up.	

COMMANDG
1/21ST LONDON REGT

WAR DIARY or INTELLIGENCE SUMMARY

Army Form C. 2118.

Vol 19

1/21st LONDON REGIMENT.

Place	Date	Hour	Summary of Events and Information	Remarks and references to Appendices
Maps Refs: BELGIUM. 28 N.W. 1/20,000 HAZEBROUCK 5A. 1/100,000	1917 MARCH 1-7		Battn in huts at SCOTTISH CAMP. General training under Brigade scheme – special instruction for specialists.	
	7	7 pm	Battn relieved LONDON IRISH in LEFT SECTION – CANAL SUB-SECTOR. Much good constructional work done. Remained, with the exception of sniping activity, were not very apparent. Patrols were sent out nightly & obtained good reports – on three no opposition was encountered except on one occasion when a large party of Germans were seen – owing to fewer numbers our patrols successfully withdrew & artillery fire was directed with good effect.	
	16	9 pm	Battn changed over with 22nd LONDON REGT and went into support – Several working parties were found.	
	22	8 pm	Battn relieved from support by 6th LONDON REGT and on relief went to SCOTTISH LINES	
	24	9.30 am	After one day for refitting etc the Battn commenced a three days trek to training area near TILQUES. First day, both billeted outside STEENVOORDE – 10 miles	
	25	9.30 am	Battn marched to ARNEKE – 11 miles	
	26	8 am	— MOULLE – 15 miles – arriving about 4.30 pm – divisions being taken on the way.	
	27-31		Training started – firstly in platoons and then by companies. News received from long period of winter well and have hardened up considerably. The three days marches, considering that the battn has done very little in the way of marching, was very good – and discipline being maintained.	

[Signature] MAJOR
COMMANDING
1/21st LONDON REGT

31-3-17

WAR DIARY or INTELLIGENCE SUMMARY

Army Form C. 2118.

21st Bn London Reg't Vol 20

1/21st LONDON REGIMENT

Ref: Maps: BELGIUM 28 NW 1/20,000 Ed.4.A. HAZEBROUCK 5a. 1/100,000

Place	Date	Hour	Summary of Events and Information	Remarks and references to Appendices
	1917 APRIL			
MOULLE	1-7		Batt'n carrying out 12 days training scheme — which was interfered with by bad weather. During this short period away from the SALIENT the health of all ranks was considerably improved.	
ARNEKE STEENVOORDE DICKIEBUSH	8-11	Starting 9am	Batt'n started the 3 days return march — spending two days in STEENVOORDE — then on marching into huts at DICKIEBUSH. H.27.b. Distance covered approximately 35 miles.	
RAVINE WOOD	12	10 p.m.	Batt'n relieved 15th LONDON REG'T in LEFT SECTION – CANAL – SUB – SECTOR. For first two nights enemy artillery and trench mortars were excessive — short bursts of shrapnel being sent intermittently on our SUPPORT – RESERVE LINES and return dumps — On the third night after a systematic and heavy retaliation by our own artillery and trench mortars the enemy was held the upper hand again. No enemy patrols was encountered by our own but on one occasion at 9 p.m. a small enemy patrol threw a few bombs into our trench at I.34.b.25.00. and were quickly dispersed. During the tour of Trenches much good constructional work was done.	
HALIFAX CAMP	19	11.30 p.m.	Batt'n relieved by 22nd LONDON REG'T and in relief moved to HALIFAX CAMP for 7 days during which time light training was carried out.	
RAVINE WOOD	27	11.45 p.m.	Batt'n relieved 22nd LONDON REG'T in LEFT SECTION – CANAL SUB. SECTOR. Systematic bombardment of enemy trenches opposite carried out – hostile artillery active laying attention chiefly to counter battery work and shelling back areas — Some retaliation was received on our own trenches	

April 30. 1917

[Signed] Lt Col Commanding
1/21st LONDON REGIMENT.

Army Form C. 2118.

WAR DIARY
or
INTELLIGENCE SUMMARY.
(Erase heading not required.)

1/21st Bn LONDON REGIMENT.

Instructions regarding War Diaries and Intelligence Summaries are contained in F.S. Regs, Part II. and the Staff Manual respectively. Title pages will be prepared in manuscript.

Place	Date	Hour	Summary of Events and Information	Remarks and references to Appendices
			Refce Maps HAZEBROUCK 5a - 1/100,000 BELGIUM 28NW - 1/20,000	
TRENCHES, LEFT SECTION CANAL SUB-SECTOR	MAY 1-4	Midnight	Battn in trenches - comparatively quiet period except for intermittent shelling of SUPPORT and RESERVE LINES - no previous reliable information and no hostile patrols were encountered. 1 casualty of 414th I.R. who deserted taken proves to be very intelligent and much information has since been obtained from him.	
HALIFAX CAMP	4	Midnight	Battn relieved by 22nd Bn LONDON RGT and on relief proceeded to HALIFAX CAMP which recently was shelled during the day & hit with the aid of aerial observation, and again on the night 5/6 May - Since this date the surrounding rest areas have been frequently shelled.	
EPERLEQUES	6	9am	Battn entrained at WIZERNHOEK - detrained at WATTEN - thence marched to EPERLEQUES for 5 days musketry range near TILQUES - during this period the shooting of the batn was considerably improved upon and the health of the Battn benefited by the change and good weather.	
COMMAGHTON PATRICIA LINES LH SECTOR - GODWAERS SECTOR	12 13	9.30am Midnight	Battn returned to divisional area - detrained at WATTEN - billeted at ANGETTE Battn relieved 22nd Bn in RAVINE WOOD sector and during this period hostile artillery was considerably more active and more guns seem to have been brought up. On afternoon 17th recently of Battn HQ's was very heavily shelled causing much local damage. There was again evidence as a result of an S.O.S. call at 9pm by batts on our left. During this period hostile aircraft were very active by 19th Bn LONDON RGT and on relief proceeded to STEENVOORDE area - entraining at ASYLUM [Alt 2 a]	
STEENVOORDE Area	20	1am	Key enemy reconnaissance flying low over our lines just before dawn.	
DOMINION LINES	24	3pm	Battn did 4 days training in "flagga" came to relieve garrisons. Battn left STEENVOORDE for Divisional area - entraining GODWAERSVELDE 5pm for BRANDHOEK G12a - arriving in camp 7pm	
LEFT SECTION CANAL SUB-SECTOR	25	Midnight	Battn relieved 19th Bn LONDON RGT — Hostile artillery again active during this period - frequent retaliating for our organised heavy bombardments - and a result of our S.O.S. by batn on our LEFT a heavy barrage on our LEFT COY area - RESERVE LINES and RAVINE followed - At night in reply to our trench searchlight scheme enemy seems to have effectively replied and in driving have known up several of our ammunition dumps. Continual hostile artillery activity on back areas continued with gas shelling	
OTTAWA CAMP	31	Midnight	Relieved by 19th Bn LONDON RGT and on relief proceeded to OTTAWA CAMP.	

A6975 Wt. W11422/M1160 350,000 12/16 D.D. & I. Forms/C./2118/14 on nights 30/31 and 31 May/1 June 1917

142/41
1/21 London
Vol 22

Army Form C. 2118.

WAR DIARY
INTELLIGENCE SUMMARY
(Erase heading not required.)

Instructions regarding War Diaries and Intelligence Summaries are contained in F. S. Regs., Pt. II. and the Staff Manual respectively. Title pages will be prepared in manuscript.

1/21 London Regiment.

Place	Date	Hour	Summary of Events and Information	Remarks and references to Appendices
			Refce Maps BELGIUM. 28 NN 1/20,000 ZILLEBEKE 1/10,000 WYTESCHAETE 1/10,000 HAZEBROUCK 5A 1/100,000	
OTTAWA CAMP	JUNE 1–4		Battalion in Ottawa Camp G.2.H.C. – busy in equipping for coming offensive.	
Woodcote House	4–5	9 pm	Batt. left Camp for Nunnery dispositions for offensive	
G.H.Q. 2nd Line	6–7		During two periods of ten days WOODCOTE HOUSE area was heavily shelled with H.E. & gas shells.	
Assembly Trenches	7th	2 am	On night 6/7 June 10 p.m. Battalion moved up to Companies nite Assembly trenches having breakfast. 2 am. on morning of 7th. [ZERO DAY OF SECOND ARMY OFFENSIVE.]	
		3.10 am	Opening of Battle of MESSINES and WYTSCHAETE – Large mines exploded by 171st 60 and ST. ELOI.	
		4.50 am	Enemy barrage opened after 1½ minutes but despite this all local objectives i.e. BLUE LINE as laid down in phase 1 were taken by 22nd & 24th London Regiments. About 30 prisoners taken and very few casualties received.	
			Opening of Battle as opportunity received batn. moved up from 1st Assembly trenches to dispositions during this line as opportunity. Few casualties in O.B. trenches – one casually only.	
		5.25 am	Companies moved up to BLUE LINE as taken by 22nd London – in extended order – in so doing about 15 casualties were incurred – including the loss of a Company Commander – intermittent shelling but no barrage	
		6.15 am	All Companies reported in position in BLUE LINE for Phase 2 of the general attack.	
		6.50 am	Leading waves left BLUE LINE where necessary to conform with direction of 1st objective	
		7 am	Battalion advanced HQrs established in QUARRY at O.S.A. 4.9	
		7.12 am	1st objective taken without difficulty. Casualties slight	
SECOND ARMY OFFENSIVE		7.30 am	Advance was continued – enemy artillery weak but considerable M.G. rifle fire from BATTLE WOOD – left flank – where 23rd Division were held up – and during any mile leads to make any further advances in Phase 2 – Conflicting reports being continually received. Efforts to let its troops & small parties who report sent to Brigade that many above dugouts attack on left has failed.	
		9.30 am	Leaders SPOIL BANK [western end] – 3rd objective – were held up. On the right of SPOIL BANK – half A Company succeeded in crossing the CANAL making for final objective. – OBLIQUE TRENCH – OBLIQUE ROW – Heavy casualties including 4 or 5 of 2 officers killed – one being a Company Commander. As there were concrete M.G. positions & several dug-outs on the SPOIL BANK still in good condition which were holding up the attack, a further bombardment was ordered by our heavy artillery – this necessitates the withdrawal of OAF LANE	
		2 pm	Bombardment commenced & lasted till 7 pm	
		7 pm	Three Companies of 20th LONDON sent up – a further attack was made on SPOIL BANK and	

Army Form C. 2118.

WAR DIARY
INTELLIGENCE SUMMARY
(Erase heading not required.)

Title: 1/21 London Regiment.

Place	Date 1917	Hour	Summary of Events and Information	Remarks and references to Appendices
	7 June	7 p.m.	(continued) Final objective being taken, Enemy immediately opened very heavy barrage. A post was established again at western end of SPOIL BANK which had to be withdrawn owing to a threatened counter attack	
		8.30 pm	from S.E. at 8.30 p.m. Two platoons of 21st had gone over in support of 20th LONDON, but together with the latter met with very heavy casualties. Estimated casualties of battalion for day's fighting 160	
	8th to night 9/10th		Battalion reformed during morning of 8th — 20th & 22nd Battalions withdrawn from BLUE LINE thereby relieving the congestion in that trench. Consolidation work in progress - Enemy sniping very heavily during night of 7/8th June but comparatively quiet during day. Our M.Gs. occasionally fired short bursts at stray parties of enemy who were showing themselves about 1500 yards away. At 4 p.m. another enemy barrage was opened during which an unsuccessful local attack was made on our left flank at BATTLE WOOD. Again at 8.30 pm a heavy barrage was opened - one of their aeroplanes having signalled that enemy were concentrating to the N. Both sides artillery continued firing until 11 p.m. during which time we had about 35 casualties. Total casualties for offensive 244.	
28 NW 1/20000 night 9/10	9th	6 p.m.	Lorry containing working party sustained direct hit by shell in YPRES - 13 killed, 11 wounded	
Belgium & France 28. Edn3 1/40,000		midnight	Battalion relieved by 19th LONDON von ARUNDEL HOUSE H33.C. relief proceeded to OLD FRENCH TRENCH and	
CAESTRE	12th	2.30 pm	Battalion marched back to HEKSKEN M.3.C. 15 miles & proceeded to re-equip where necessary.	
	14th	5 p.m.	Battalion proceeded by march route to CAESTRE, arrived 9 p.m. - billeting for the night.	
SERCUS	15th	7.30 am	Battalion marched to SERCUS - arriving about 11 a.m. During the stay ordinary light training was undertaken, special attention being paid to re-organisation of platoons & training up specialists as required. Training was done between 5.30 & 10 am	
METEREN	27th	6 am.	Battalion marched to METEREN, 12 miles, & billetted on arrival.	
RIDGEWOOD	28th	5 am.	Battalion marched to bivouacs at H.35.d. - arriving 11.30 am	
ST ELOI	29	11 pm	Relieved 32nd ROYAL FUSILIERS — 41st DIVN — in LEFT SECTION - RIGHT BDE — 2nd LONDON on RIGHT - 13th MIDDLESEX on left - Trenches in bad condition owing to weather.	
	30		Bad weather but beyond intermittent sharp enemy artillery swept.	

Arthur McKenna
Lt Col
Commdg. 1/21 LONDON BATT.

SCALE 1/20,000.

Message

...............DIVISION.
Map reference
or Mark on Map
at back.

1. My {Company / Platoon} has reached..............
2. My {Company / Platoon} is at.............. and is consolidating.
3. My {Company / Platoon} is at..............and has consolidated.
4. Am held up by M.G. at..............
5. I need :— Ammunition.
   Bombs.
   Rifle Grenades.
   Water.
   Very lights.
   Stokes shells.
6. Counter attack forming up at..............
7. I am in touch with.............. on Right at.............. Left
8. I am not in touch with.............. on Right / Left
9. I am being shelled from..............
10. I estimate my present strength at..............rifles.
11. Hostile {Battery / Machine Gun / Trench Mortar} active at..............

Time.. 4. p. m.
Date.. 11/4/17....

Name... C.H. Edwards 2/Lt.
Platoon........ 7.
Company........ "B"
Battalion.... 1/2st Lond. Regt.

Army Form W. 3091.

Cover for Documents.

Nature of Enclosures.

Report on Operations of 21st Bn.
London Regt.
on
7d June 1917

Notes, or Letters written.

SECRET.

142nd Inf Bde

Please render a report in detail of the operations carried out by the 21st Battalion during attack on morning of the 7th inst; also of the minor enterprise carried out on the evening of the 7th inst. Reports by each surviving platoon commander to be attached, giving action taken by his platoon and marking in positions of platoons during various stages. Casualties etc to be added.

The Divisional Commander also desires the opinion of the Brigadier General as to reasons why the attack failed.

AJT.

Lt.Colonel,
General Staff,
47th (London) Division.

GX.3/51
10th June 1917.

CONFIDENTIAL.

142nd Infantry Brigade.

Reference the report contained in your M.50 dated 14-6-17:

I concur with the opinion of the G.O.C. 142nd Infantry Brigade — as regards the attack by the 21st Bn. in the 2nd Phase on the morning of the 7th June

In the case of

(a) 2nd Lieut. BARKER — The order to retire from the spoil bank appears to have been given to Nos. 9 and 11 Platoons by 2nd Lieut. BARKER on his own responsibility, apparently because he had received no reinforcements after 30 or 40 minutes.

(b) Capt. ENGLISH who, it is understood, gave the orders to the Company (2nd Lt. JACKMAN) to retire at 9.45 a.m. on his own responsibility.

Both of these Officers (Captain ENGLISH and 2nd Lieut. BARKER) are to be informed that their action appears to have been entirely unjustified, and they will accordingly be called upon to furnish a full explanation of their reasons for issuing orders to retire.

Major General,
Commanding 47th (London) Division.

G.X/3/52.
21st June, 1917.

M 50 returned to 142 Bde attached to above letter.

Report of Operations of 11th June 1917 No 5 Platoon B Coy on the morning of the 7th June

Objectives: portion of Our Line & O.B. & Part of Oblique Row

The platoon was in position in Assembly trenches in front of S.P.7. on the night of the 6th June. At 4-15 AM on the 7th the platoon left for the OB line arriving at 5-0 A.M. Left OB line at 5-35 AM. About the second German line a party of the enemy numbering about twenty surrendered and were left for waves following to deal with. At this point platoon lost direction slightly to the right but recovered and got into position slightly in advance of the Blue line at 6-15 AM. At this point the attack came under fire from Machine Guns & Snipers apparently from the direction of Battle Wood and suffered the first casualties. The platoon left the Blue line at 6-55 AM. and arrived at a Trench slightly to the North of Our Lane at

7-15 AM. Oaf Lane was in a very bad condition and after sending forward a small party who reported the ground to be clear, I decided to consolidate the trench about fifteen yards to the North of Oaf Lane. I was in touch with the platoon of "A" Company on my right and reported my position and casualties, which amounted to five, to advanced Batt. HQ at 7-45 AM. About 7.30 AM I sent a party of men under Cpl Webb with instructions to report to the Officer i/c the Left platoon who appeared to be loosing rather heavily.

AM Woodruff 2/Lt
O.C. 5 Platoon B. Coy.

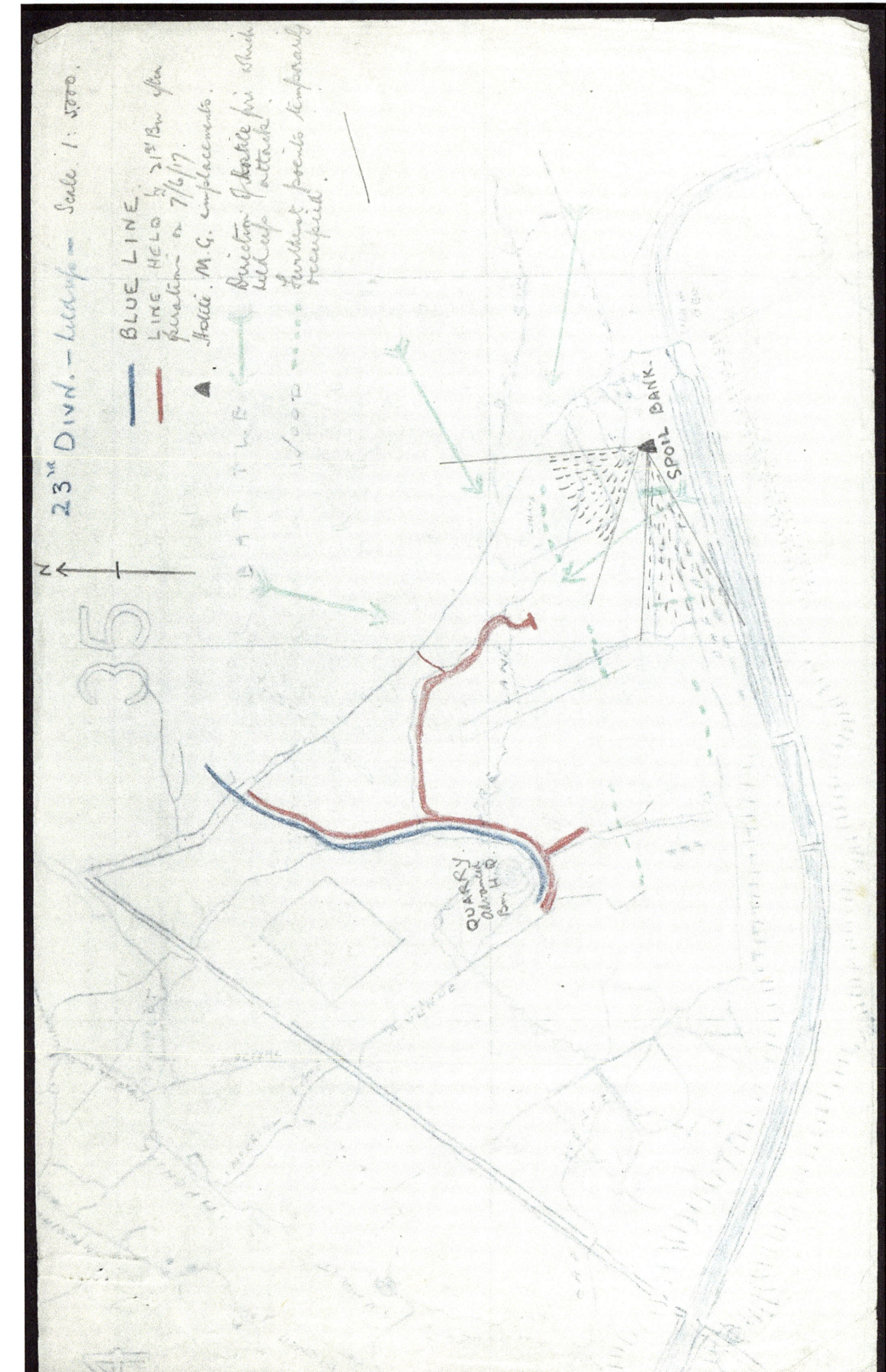

Confidential

Headquarters,
47th. (London) Division.

1. With reference to your G.X. 3/52 dated June 10th., a report of the operations on June 7th by O.C. 21st. London Regt. is forwarded herewith, also a report by O.C. 20th. London Regt. regarding the minor enterprise undertaken by three companies of this battalion on the evening of the 7th June.

Reports by surviving platoon commanders of the 21st. London Regt. are attached as directed, and casualties for both operations are stated in the Battalion Commanders reports.

2. In my opinion the reasons for the failure of the attack by the 21st. London Regt. were –

(a) The left flank of this battalion was exposed during practically the whole operation.

(b) The attacking troops were subjected to heavy machine gun fire from the EASTERN END of the SPOIL BANK at about O.5.b.5.6. and BATTLE WOOD, and the enemy's snipers caused considerable casualties to the third and fourth waves of the attack.

(c) That C and D Companies had both their company commanders killed shortly after the attack was launched.

I consider, however, that more determination might have been shown in pushing the attack home to the final objective, bearing in mind that the battalion had not, in my opinion, suffered excessive casualties which would have rendered the re-organization and weight of attack inadequate.

I also consider that it was an error of judgment not to have attempted to hold on to and consolidate OBLIQUE ROW (NORTH of the CANAL), and the West end of SPOIL BANK, which points appear to have been gained without undue loss.

3. As regards the minor enterprise carried out by troops of the 20th Battalion at 7 p.m. June 7th., supported by two platoons of 21st. Battalion, I consider that the causes of failure of this attack were -

- (a) A very heavy hostile barrage was placed on our troops at the moment of deployment for the attack.

- (b) Two platoons of the left company appear to have lost direction and this fact militated against the pre-arranged plan of attack.

- (c) The hostile machine gun fire from the SPOIL BANK does not appear to have been affected by the re-bombardment, and still caused considerable casualties to the attacking troops.

I consider that it was an error of judgment on the part of Captain ADAMS that he did not endeavour to retain his foothold on the objectives he had reached.

V. T. Bailey
Brig. Genl. comdg.
142nd. Inf. Bde.

M50.
14/6/17.

1/21st LONDON REGT.

REPORT ON PART taken by BATT'N in OPERATIONS of June 7th – 9th

Refce Map No 3A 1:5000

Z Day

3.10 am.	In assembly trenches
5.15 am.	In position in old front line system.
5.25 am.	Leading wave left front line in extended order, others in succession.
5.45 am.	Party of about 30 germans found in a hollow between O.G.1. + O.G.2. They surrendered and were sent back under escort.
6.15 am.	All waves in position in BLUE LINE
6.50 am.	Waves started forward & got into position close up to Barrage.
7.0 am.	B'n Advanced HQ under Capt English established in Quarry at O.5.a.40.95.
7.12 am.	1st Objective taken without difficulty. Casualties up to now very slight
7.30 am.	Received report from B'n Intelligence Officer that advance was being continued with very little enemy artillery but that troops were encountering considerable M.G & rifle fire from direction of BATTLE WOOD.
	From this time no reports were received as to our movements although every effort was made to get into touch with our waves.
9.5 am.	Received information from Bde that 23rd Div'n were held up at IMPARTIAL TRENCH and IMPACT TERRACE but this was almost immediately contradicted & I was informed that the 23rd Div'n were almost up to their BLACK LINE.
9.10 am.	As there was still no news coming in, I sent 2nd LT. HOLLAND forward to get all possible information & report back without delay
9.15 am.	Information received from left of 2nd wave that they had met with heavy M.G. + rifle fire & were unable to get on. This was confirmed by O/c B Coy who reported that he could not get beyond trench at O.5.b.35.75. owing to this fire.
9.30 am.	After consultation with the B.G.C. I, acting on his orders, went forward to advanced H.Q. After consultation with Capt ENGLISH & seeing all available runners etc, I reported that, so far as I could ascertain, the attack had completely failed on the left owing to M.G + rifle fire from EASTERN end of SPOIL BANK + from the direction of OAF KEEP.

On the right however some small parties had managed to get to the western end of the bank & were astride it. But they also could not get on owing to a M.G. in an undamaged emplacement. The B.G.C. asked me whether if I were reinforced by 2 Coys of fresh troops, there would be a reasonable prospect of a fresh attack being successful. I replied 'yes' but that I should prefer a further artillery preparation. On this report it was arranged that a Coy of the 20th London should be sent to me & that I was to make all arrangements for launching a further organised attack on the SPOIL BANK & the objective on the South bank of the CANAL, with this Coy plus such men of my own unit as I could muster, and about 100 men of the 22ND LONDON under CAPT HAMILTON. Later however, as the result of a report from my I.O. & my own observation on the ground I informed the B.G.C that in my opinion the fire was too severe for the attack to be successful & that further bombardment was essential. He then ordered me to await further orders & in the meantime to continue consolidation of the line we were holding. Subsequently I had orders from the B.G.C that a rebombardment of the SPOIL BANK would take place starting about 2 pm & that I was to withdraw all troops in advance of OAF LANE to that line & to continue consolidation there. I accordingly withdrew my troops from the SPOIL BANK & OBLIQUE ROW & awaited further orders with regard to the attack to be attempted later.

At about 1.30 pm I reported personally at the 142 Bde HQ & saw the B.G.C who informed me that a minor operation would take place that evening, the zero hour being 7 pm after a bombardment of the SPOIL BANK by our heavy guns. The attack would be carried out by 3 Coys of the 20th Battn (Col Matthews) & that I was to render such assistance & support as was required.

I saw Col. Matthews, and his Operation Orders with those issued by the 142 Bde are attached. With regard to this Operation, immediately prior to Zero, Capt MOLL (who was in charge of the 20th Battn Advanced HQ) asked me for 2 platoons to support his attack on the SOUTH side of the CANAL & these I detailed from my D Coy, under 2 Lt JACKMAN. At 7 pm, the hour fixed for this attack a very heavy hostile barrage was opened on our lines & advance was impossible. With regard to the NORTH bank, a small party of the 20th managed to establish a post on the western end of the SPOIL BANK & on receiving information of this, I arranged to reinforce them with a company of the 21st BATTN. Before this could be done however I heard from this post, from my left Coy Commander & by means of an aeroplane light (this was about 8.30 pm) that a hostile attack appeared to be imminent from the S.E. In view of this I considered it inadvisable to send men forward from my line, and, as the post was a small one only, ordered it to withdraw. As a matter of fact a very severe hostile barrage was opened on my front line at 8.40 pm, though no actual attack materialised on my immediate front.

The foregoing is from information at my disposal on Z day. The following I have ascertained by enquiry since from officers & NCOs.

The first objective was gained without trouble, but beyond this line each succeeding wave came under heavy rifle & M.G fire from three directions namely:—

    a) Eastern End of SPOIL BANK
    b) Direction of OAF KEEP
    c) From left & left rear in BATTLE WOOD.

This fire & made advance across the open impossible & efforts were made to advance by means of shell holes and any trenches running towards SPOIL BANK.

Slight progress was made in this way, and the Collars & OBLIQUE ROW (North of Canal) were found to be unoccupied. Beyond this further progress was impossible.

On the right progress was made to the Short trench at O.5a.70.50. when troops also came under crossfire. A portion of the 2nd wave managed to push on to SPOIL BANK & tried to push along the top to the Eastern end. In the meantime the third wave seeing the second wave held up, pushed on in an effort to carry them forward, but they too came under the same fire, & only isolated parties were able to get forward. At 8.25 am, we had a line across the top of the bank but we could not carry the line down either side owing to the M.G. fire from both North & South. The Eastern end of the bank was strongly held & the M.G. emplacements there were intact & occupied. The furthest point occupied by us appears to have been the trench immediately west of the S in OAF STREET. A small gun position was found at this point, but there was no gun. Each succeeding wave appears to have made every effort to support those in front, & the fourth wave continued its advance, but even with this assistance the line could not be carried forward. At about 8.45 am efforts were made by 2ND LTS WALLIS & DEANE (both of whom were killed) with a party of men to get across the CANAL with a view to assisting from that side. But although they got across, they could not advance beyond the Southern bank owing again to rifle & M.G. fire. This party withdrew at 9.15 am under orders from

2ND LT BARKER who had joined them & who appears to have tried hard to get on towards the final objective. At 9.30 am Capt PERNMS made further attempts to get to our BLACK LINE but again without success. He was hit in this attempt.

The attached map shows in pencil the furthest points reached by the unit under my command & in RED the line we consolidated.

A Day. Consolidation was continued but much hindered by continual damage by hostile bombardments. In the evening the 20th Batn troops were withdrawn.

B Day. On the morning of B Day the 22nd Batn withdrew from the BLUE LINE which this was then occupied by me. On the night of B/C we were relieved by the 19th Batn London Regt & withdrew to old FRENCH TRENCH where we are now.

My total casualties were 5 officers & 234 O.R, & of these the majority occurred between OAF LANE & the SPOIL BANK.

At no time during the operations were we properly in touch with the 69th Bde on our LEFT but communication was always kept with the BATTNS on our right.

I regret that the BATTN under my command was unable to gain all its objectives but I consider under the circumstances it was impossible to do so for the following reasons.

    a) The 69th Bde did not get forward & so my left flank was completely exposed.
    b) M.G emplacements on the SPOIL BANK were intact & occupied.

These two causes exposed my troops to very heavy fire from front left, & left rear in the advance beyond OAF LANE & it was between here & the SPOIL BANK, that the majority of my casualties occurred.

Field
11/4/17

SECRET.   Copy No. 7

142nd. INFANTRY BRIGADE

Operation Order No. 186.

Ref. Map - No. S.A (47th. Div.) dated
30/5/17.   June 7th., 1917.

1. The 21st. Lon. Regt. has not yet gained the 2nd., 3rd. and 4th objectives of the Second phase of Second Army Offensive allotted to it.

2. The G.O.C. 142nd. Inf. Bde. has decided to resume the attack on the objectives not captured by 21st. Battn.

3. The objectives are as follows -
   (a) Spoil Bank from O.5.a.8.3. to O.5.b.8.6.
   (b) OBLIQUE ROW.
   (c) OPAL RESERVE from O.5.c.8.7. to O.5.d.2.8.
        (junction of OBLIQUE ROW and OPAL RESERVE.)

4. The assault will take place at 7 p.m. on June 7th., and will be made by 20th. London Regt., less one company, supported by 21st. London Regt.
    O. C. 20th. London Regt. will be in command of the attack and will make all detailed arrangements.
    Of the three companies of the 20th. London Regt., one company has already moved forward and is at present with 21st. London Regt. The second and third companies will move forward under orders to be issued by O.C. 20th. London Regt. so as to reach their assembly places by 6.40 p.m. June 7th.

5. An intense artillery bombardment by heavy artillery will be carried out from 2.30 p.m. to 6.55 p.m. on the SPOIL BANK, OBLIQUE ROW and OPAL RESERVE.

6. The attack will be made generally from the line O.5.c.6.8. to the QUARRY O.5.a.4.9. in an Easterly direction, one company advancing SOUTH of the CANAL and two companies NORTH of the CANAL.

7. A creeping barrage will cover the advance of the attacking troops. This barrage will move at the rate of 100 yards per five minutes. It will commence at 6.55 p.m. and lift off the SPOIL BANK, OBLIQUE ROW at 7 p.m. to enable the infantry to assault at that hour.

                                                    Captain,
                                                    Bde. Major,
Issued to Signals at 4.35 p.m.   142nd. Inf. Bde.

Copy No. 1. War Diary.
       2. File.
       3. 21st.Lon.
       4. 22nd.Lon.
       5. 23rd.Lon.
       6. 24th.Lon.
       7. 20th. Lon.
       8. 141st.Inf.Bde.
       9. 140th. Inf. Bde.
      10. 47th. Divn.
      11. 69th. Bde.
      12. 142nd.T.M.Bty.
      13. 142nd.T.M.Bty.

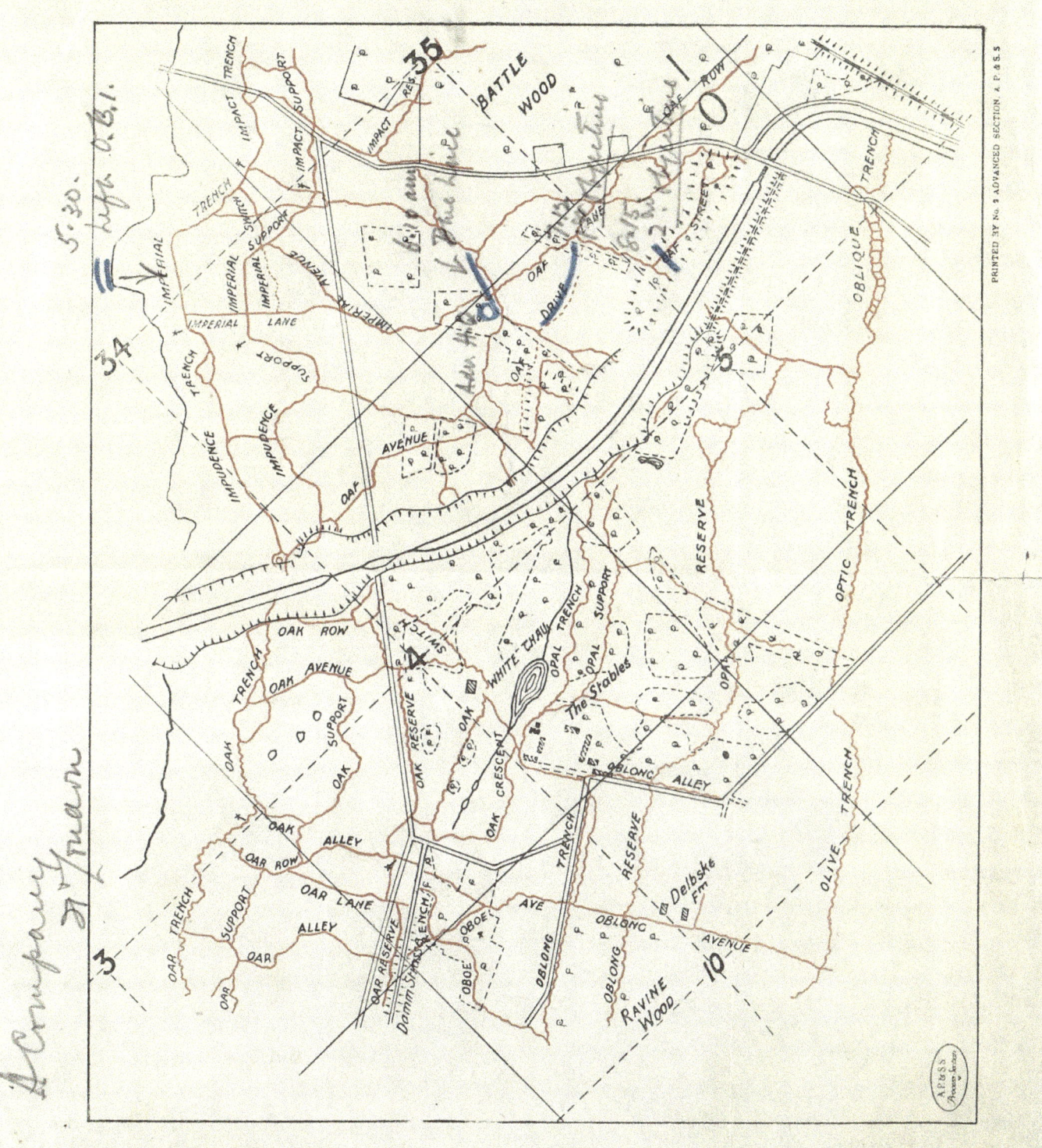

.... DIVISION
Map reference or
Mark on MAP on
Back.

1. I am at..........
2. I am at.......... and am consolidating
3. I am at.......... and have consolidated
4. Am held up by M.G. at..........
5. I need :- Ammunition
             Bombs
             Rifle Grenades
             Water
             Very Lights
             Stokes shells
6. Counter attack forming up at..........
7. I am in touch with.......... on RIGHT at.......... on LEFT
8. I am not in touch on RIGHT / LEFT
9. Am being shelled from..........
10. I estimate my present strength at.......... rifles
11. Hostile { BATTERY / MACHINE GUN / TRENCH MORTAR } active at..........

Time..........m   Name..........
Date..........   Platoon..........
                  Company..........
                  Battalion..........

Report of Operations of No 6 Platoon
"B" Coy on the morning of
7th June. 1917.

Objective Cellars in O.5.b + portion of Bof lane adjoining

4-30 a.m. Left assembly trench in front of S.P.7

5. 0 a.m. Arrived in position in O.B.1

5-35 a.m. Left O.B.1. The platoon lost direction slightly to the right after leaving O.G.2.

6-15 a.m. Arrived in Blue line. Got in touch with 9th Yorks in Battle Wood. Had casualties here. Heavy rifle and machine gun fire. Reported to Officer of 9th Yorks that we were weak but he could give us no men.

6-55 a.m. Left Blue Line to assault by the cellars. Machine gun and rifle fire continuously through our own barrage. More casualties bringing total to about half platoon. Lewis Gun Section

Report of Operations of No 1 Platoon
of B. Coy on the morning of June 7·17

At 4·20 AM I left Assembly Trench S.P.7
5 AM I arrived at O.B.1
6·20 AM Arrived at B.L. with 10 Men
having had casualties through
heavy Machine Gun fire & Snipers
At this point my L.M.G team
lost its direction.

6·25 AM Formed up slightly in advance
of B.L. under heavy Machine Gun
fire my casualties at this point
were 4.
At this point O.C B Coy took
charge of remainder of Platoon.

Butler R.W.
Sgt

11 June 1917.

Report of Operations of No. 7 Platoon
'B' Coy 1/21st London Regt. on the morning
of 7 June 1917.

1. The Platoon left our assembly trenches
in front of S.P.7 at 4.20 A.M. and
advanced to our position in O.B.1.
   Two casualties during this advance.
We arrived at O.B.1 at 5.5 A.M.

2. We left O.B.1 at 5.35 A.M. and advanced
towards the Blue Line which we reached
at 6.20 A.M. We failed to find any
troops occupying the Blue Line.
We formed up slightly in advance of the
Blue Line at about 6.25 A.M. At this
point my Lewis Gun Section was ordered to
be attached to No.6 Platoon by O.C. Coy.

3. From this position we started to advance
towards OAF LANE at 6.55 A.M. Here we
came under fire from machine guns and
snipers, and had about three casualties.

4. We arrived at a trench slightly North
of OAF LANE at about 7.15 A.M. Owing to

2.

the very broken nature of the ground the bombing section on the right lost direction and did not arrive at this point in time.

5. At 7.25 A.M. I started to advance towards SPOIL BANK with about 7 men, the remnants of the sections of Riflemen and Rifle Bombers. I got into touch with about 12 men on my right belonging to A, C, & D Coys, and took them forward with me. The fire from machine guns and snipers coming from the direction of BATTLE WOOD and SPOIL BANK was so severe that it was impossible to advance far. Many of the men with me became casualties, and eventually we withdrew to OAF LANE and helped in the consolidation of that position.

C. H. Edmunds 2/Lt.

O.C. 7 Platoon.

15th Platoon A Coy 7 June 1917

4:10 Left assembly trench for front line system - 1 casualty

5:30 am Left front line for Blue line in 3rd wave of Battn, nearing B.L came under Machine Gun and Snipers fire - 1 casualty

6-5 am Reached Blue line & reorganised

7-10 Left Blue line and reached first objective under heavy M.G.F.

7-40 On left being held up we passed through the first wave & made for Spoilbank which was to be taken at 7-44. 0 casualties in getting across

9-45 Received orders to withdraw to first objective and consolidate - 3 casualties in doing this

H.A Mills Lieut

from Shell Hole to Shell Hole, the enemy fire being considerable. The losses of the two platoons at this period would be about 2 killed & 3 wounded. At 7.20 A.M. 1st objective was left & advance continued during which time enemy fire from same source seemed to be of greater volume & so much so that it was impossible to continue the advance except by incurring severe casualties. At 7.45 A.M. together with a small party of about 12 including a Lewis gun a rush was made for the SPOIL BANK in support of a party of our own troops who had gained west end of it. On arrival of bank we came under the fire of strong party of Germans firing from EAST end of SPOIL BANK. Fire was

A Coy No 1 & 3 Platoons

6.30 AM Left O.B.1 as the 1st wave and proceeded in extended order towards BLUE LINE

5.40 AM Had reached to about O.9.2 when a party of Germans in number about fifteen or twenty rushed from a dugout on right and surrendered.

6.10 AM Reached Blue Line without casualties

7. AM Gained objective. Came under heavy M.G. fire from the direction of BATTLE WOOD. Snipers were also firing from BATTLE WOOD Casualties three wounded.

D Coy F.S.R.

Report of proceedings during first stage of attack on Z day.

4.10a Left assembly trenches for front line system.

5.30a Left front line system for BLUE LINE, which was reached under heavy M.G. & sniping fire

6.5a Reached BLUE LINE. Fire coming from BATTLE WOOD + EAST end of SPOILBANK

7.10a Left Blue line & got into first objective & passed through it.

7.40a A rush was made, as our left had been held up, for the SPOILBANK, which was to be taken at 7.47a. The WEST end of the Bank was reached & the party worked along towards the EAST end. Considerable

7.40 am

Seeing that the left was held up a rush was made for the Spoil Bank frontally & by getting up round the gap between the two Banks with 9 casualties

At 9.45 am received orders to withdraw from Spoil Bank to first objective & to consolidate 4 more casualties

Signed
A Webb
Sgt.

7/6.17.

Report on operations of B Coy. 1/21st London Regt on Morning of June 7th 17.

1. The Company commenced leaving assembly trench in front of S P 9 at about 4.15 AM & were in position in OB1 at 5.0 AM, sustaining 5 Casualties during this advance.

2. Left OB1 at 5.35 AM and advanced to Blue Line, reaching this at about 6.20 AM. It was ~~probably~~ impossible to exactly fix the position of the Blue Line on our left as there were no men seen on this flank.

3. Owing to No 8 Platoon losing its direction to the right I ordered No 7 Platoon Lewis Gun team to work to the left & cover No 6 Platoon's flank on BATTLE WOOD.

Immediately on leaving the Blue Line

objective was so severe recruits that they had to return to the C.T. & hold an position there.

I reported to O.C Battn advanced H.Q. where I was & how held up.

I was unable to get into touch with the 69th Brigade on our left after having left the Blue Line, as there appeared to be only a few isolated bodies of men in BATTLE WOOD, who afterwards withdrew to about 200 yds in rear of our position.

Shawton ?/Lt
9. B Coy.

had got detached, and O.C. Coy attached J Platoon L.G Section to cover left flank. During our advance observed men of Battⁿ on left in Battle Wood withdrawing.

7.45. Arrived in front of cellars but owing to heavy fire and small number of men (about eight) and no supporting waves, decided to occupy trench on our right. In this trench we touched with our No 5 Platoon, under Mr Woodruffe, and commenced consolidating same immediately.

J Bockett (No 650463)
L/Sergt No 6 Platoon
10/6/17

We were also held up by Machine Gun fire from the top of Spoil Bank left and rifle fire from Battle Wood.

We reached a point O5a 80.90 with 10 men and were unable to advance further. Our casualties were, one killed and six wounded.

I reported from this point to advanced H.Q.

At 9.0.n I withdrew to the trench where B Coy were consolidating, losing one killed and one wounded.

Reported from here to advanced H.Q. & received orders to remain in trench and consolidate.

J. M. Allison 2/Lt.
O.C. 12 Platoon.
(MOPPING UP)

No.10 Platoon, C. Coy
(Moppers up)

Left Assembly Trench at 4.15 a.m (One man wounded)
Advanced through the barrage & took up position in Woolley Walk at 5.10 & collected the platoon.
Left O.B.1 at 5.35 a.m.
Arrived on the Blue Line at 6.20 a.m (Platoon Sergeant & 1 man wounded)
Got into touch with No.12 Platoon
At 7.45 seeing troops detailed to attack the Spoil Bank held up in front decided in conjunction with O/C No.12 Platoon to advance against the Spoil Bank.
Proceeded to do so under heavy machine gun & rifle fire through O.5 Lane to O.5 a 80,90. A bullet pierced a M.S.K barrel & affected several men, two of whom subsequently went to the Aid Post. One man killed & senior n.c.o wounded.
Held up by machine gun & rifle fire

of 6 Coy and moved up with No 9 & 11 Platoons towards OAK LANE. Again came under heavy fire. Three casualties occurring at about I 35. C 65.10. As preceding waves could not get on I moved up via cutting to Western end of SPOIL BANK and joined D Coy. Having reconnoitred this end of Bank Sgt Hocking went forward with patrol to reconnoitre E. end of SPOIL BANK.

At 8.45 am 2 Lt DEAN decided to cross CANAL and join up with Right Batt. who had crossed CANAL lower down.

Immediately on crossing we came under very severe MG & rifle fire

About eight reached half way up bank. Of these four were hit including 2 Lt WALLIS. The remainder took cover and were kept down by intense fire

I sent back message explaining situation but getting no reinforcements gave instructions after 30 or 40 minutes

right of the light railway, with the intention of crossing towards the SNOUT, south of canal. Received much opposition on Shrethbank with snipers and M. Guns, and withdrew under orders about 9.45 to first objective which we consolidated. 2 casualties in withdrawing

Jas. M. R. Pope
Plat. 878

20/30 enemy crawling towards us. We also came under machine gun fire from our right front apparently from position on bank across the Canal. Here we got help from some of A Coy but had to withdraw owing to the machine gun and rifle fire from both flanks leaving several casualties. I then reported to 2nd Lt Barker receiving orders to await further instructions. Later received orders to consolidate.

P.J. Hockney Sgt
11 Platoon

Spoil Bank + a position on
our right flank.
Casualties about 6

7.30. 2nd wave left 1st objective
+ proceeded to 2nd objective
but were unable to get on owing
to barrage failing to lift.
M.G. + rifle fire was very active
during the whole of this time
from the same points as above
We engaged the snipers on Spoil
Bank with Lewis Gun fire.
Casualties about 6

8.16.
A party of our own troops were
seen to have gained the Spoil Bank
from the W. End.
It was decided to send a party up
to support them, which was done.
This party reconnoitred the top of
the Spoil Bank on the W. End +
found no enemy

11 Platoon, C. Company
Details of battle movements on Z day.

We left assembly trench at 4.15 a.m and moved up to front line system leaving at 5.35 a.m. We advanced to our position in the Blue line. After advancing about 50 yds I received orders from 2nd Lt Barker to proceed with him to join D Coy at Eastern end of Spoil Bank. Until now my casualties were nil. We then advanced behind our own barrage as far as the ridge at 8.15 a.m. Here we were divided into two parties one remaining with 2nd Lt Barker and the other I took along the ridge reconnoitring dugouts, etc. and if possible to get into touch with the people on our left. About half way along the ridge we encountered machine gun fire from our left front and I ordered my men to take cover whilst I went forward with a Corporal along the ridge passing one or two broken down dugouts and also an old field gun position. Just past these and about 50/60 yds ahead of us we saw between

7.30 AM Sent Cpl Mullens out for purposes of Reconnaissance. On the right flank we were in touch with 24th Batt.

8.15 AM Consolidated and Strengthened position. Reported to Capt. English as ? having gained my objective.

R V Dell
2/Lt.
19s Platoon

From 2nd Lieut Mr. H. E. FRANSHAM
i/c 2nd Wave of "A" Coy. (Nos 2 Y 4 Platoons)

Our front line RAT ALLEY to THORNE ST. was left at 5.35 A.M. the second wave being about 50 yds. in rear of first. Movement forward was checked between O.G. 1 y 2 for about 3 minutes by the sudden exit of some 15 or 20 Germans from a concrete dugout with their hands up. As soon as they were disposed of the advance was continued without interruption as far as the Blue Line which was reached at 6.10 A.M. At this time it was noticed that Machine Gun rifle fire was being opened up from the left flank & came from the direction of BATTLE WOOD & the first two emplacements on top of the SPOIL BANK.

At 7 am BLUE LINE was left & advance continued by short rushes

also directed upon us from the other side of canal. Their position could not be detected. Messages were sent back to Capt ENGLISH telling him of our position at 8.48 A.M. Orders were received at 11 A.M. to withdraw which was carried out after some delay due to the disposal of wounded. Whilst there we were joined by odd parties of C & D Coys. making a total of about 20. Our casualties whilst on the SPOIL BANK were 3 killed & 4 wounded.

A.H.E. Fransham
2/Lt

13 Platoon   "D" Coy.

7.6.17

4.10 am
Left assembly trench for front line system

5.30 am Left front line system for Blue Line in 4th wave of the Batt.

6.5 am
Arrived in Blue Line with 2 casualties. Heavy M.G. & sniping fire from Battle Wood & East of Spoil Bank.

7.10 am
Left Blue Line & made for first objective 4 casualties. Re-organised there & passed through & discovered that the left of the line had been held up by M.G. & sniping fire.

From O.C. C Coy
To The Adjutant   11-6-17

MAP
REF   Report of operations Z day.

No 9 Platoon left assembly trenches at
4-15 am and took up position in
WOOLEY WALK. Sgt Baker and one
Rifleman becoming casualties between
these points.
    Reported to Capt English at OB1 at
5.25 am. Left OB1 at 5.35 am and
advanced to Blue Line.
    I moved up with D Coy (to whom No 9 was
attached) on my right. 2nd Lieut Joel
joining up on my left with No 11 Platoon
(1) at I 35 C 65 25. No other casualties
occurred up to this point which was
reached at 6.30 am although under
heavy M.G. + rifle fire from Spoil Bank &
BATTLE WOOD.
    Before moving off at 6.50 am 2nd Lieut Joel
was killed. I then took over command

opposition was met by a large party of Germans, who inflicted casualties on us with Machine Guns sweeping fire.

9.45a. Orders were received to withdraw from the SPOILBANK to the first objective & there consolidate.

Sniping & M.G. fire was still heavy from the same directions, & also H.E. Shrapnel.

Iv. W. Jackman 2/4
O.C. "D" Coy

3. The Company came under heavy machine gun & snipers fire, sustaining a good many casualties.

4. At 7.15 AM the leading wave reached its objective, i.e. The Cellars, & a portion of OAF LANE. The Platoon on the left taking the Cellars found it impossible to proceed over the open ground, owing to fire from BATTLE WOOD & Sº POIL BANK so worked into the C.T. & down that to the Cellars. These were found unoccupied & completely smashed.

5. The Second wave advancing towards the position occupied by the first wave came under such severe M.G. & Shrapnel fire that it was impossible to proceed, & as our numbers appeared now to be very small I ordered them to hold & consolidate the C.T. running down to OAF LANE.
The fire on the first wave in its

for party to return singly. Heavy
shrapnel was making position
untenable.
  Party returned two casualties
occurring in N° 11 Platoon others in
D Coy.
  In meantime N° 9 Platoon had
three casualties and N° 11 two casualties
at W. end Spoil bank. about O.S.A. 70. 40-50
  I reported to Advanced B" HQ at 10.15
receiving instructions later to consolidate

J C Barker
2 Lt
C Coy

REPORT ON MOVEMENT OF
12 PLATOON (MOPPERS UP.)
DURING OPERATIONS 6th June 1917.
_____

At 4.15 a.m. we left the assembly trench and proceeded to the front line at the top of Petticoat Lane arriving at 5 a.m.

At 5.35 a.m. we left the front line and took up our position in the Blue Line at I.36.c.50.20 at 6.45 a.m.

We left the Blue Line at 7. a.m.

Seeing the troops attacking Spoil Bank, held up I decided to support them together with O.C. No 10 Platoon

1st Platoon

4:10 — Left assembly trench for front line system

5:30 — Left front line for Blue line in 3rd wave of Battn.

6:5 — Arrived Blue line and re-organised — one casualty

7:10 — Left Blue line under considerable M.G. sniping & shrapnel fire for first objective — 5 casualties and passed through it.

7:40 — Knowing that Spoilbank was due to be taken at 7:43 and that the left was held up, a rush was made towards the Western end of the bank. received 4 casualties. The O.C. Platoon who was killed, evidently took some of the Platoon on the Spoilbank

At 9·am seeing some of our troops on Spoil
Bank again endeavoured to join them &
reached 05 a 80,70. Again held up by
machine gun rifle fire from east end of
Spoil Bank & Ruttle Wood.
Withdrew to 05 a 50,90 & reported at
10 a.m to Advance Battalion Headquarters
that I was unable to proceed. Ordered to
withdraw & consolidate.
Collected stragglers & commenced to consolidate
Subsequently found L G section & others
had lost touch & had been absorbed into
other detachments

W J Squibb
2nd Lieut

Operations by A. Coy. 21st London R.

5.30 am.
Coy. left front line (O.B.1) in two lines.
1. 3 Platoons Front Line
2. 4 " 2nd line

At O.G.2 from a large concrete dug-out about 15 Germans came out & surrendered.
These were collected in a large shell hole.
The Company continued to advance.
Casualties about 2.

6.10 am
Company in position in blue line

6.50 am
First wave left B. Line and at 7. am. assaulted his first objective which was gained with small opposition, with exception of M.G. fire & rifle fire from Battle Wood.

Proceeding eastwards along the Spoil Bank a strong party of Germans opened fire with a M.G. & rifle fire.

Our party then took cover & engaged the enemy with our Lewis Gun & rifle grenades but were unable to get around his flanks owing to M.G. fire from Battle Wood and rifle fire from the enemy side of the Canal.

We sent back for ammunition & instructions and at about 11.30 am received orders to withdraw to the first objective. This was accomplished after suffering casualties of 3 killed & 4 wounded.

11.5.17.

J B Britten 2/Lt
i/c A Coy

Message

..........DIVISION.
Map reference
or Mark on Map
at back.

1. My {Company / Platoon} has reached..............
2. My {Company / Platoon} is at.............. and is consolidating.
3. My {Company / Platoon} is at.............. and has consolidated.
4. Am held up by M.G. at..............
5. I need :—Ammunition.
   Bombs.
   Rifle Grenades.
   Water.
   Very lights.
   Stokes shells.
6. Counter attack forming up at..............
7. I am in touch with.............. on {Right / Left} at..............
8. I am not in touch with.............. on {Right / Left}
9. I am being shelled from..............
10. I estimate my present strength at.............. rifles.
11. Hostile {Battery / Machine Gun / Trench Mortar} active at..............

Time.......... m.   Name..............
Date..............   Platoon..............
                      Company..............
                      Battalion..............

G/!
After the operation
on the 7: a letter
was sent to Capt.
about Caplin.
ENGLISH 21. Dec

My I please see
it...
Returned
14/7/17   [initials]

No letter was written to
the Capt — but the J.O.C. wrote
the attached letter to 14/2
Capt.

CONFIDENTIAL.

Headquarters,

    47th. (London) Division.
_____

The attached reports by Captain English and 2nd. Lieut. Barker are forwarded as directed in G.X. 3/52 dated June 21st.

A report by O.C. 21st. London Regt. is also attached.

                      Lieut. Col. comdg.

                      142nd. Inf. Bde.

25/6/17.

G.S. have seen

    A.T.

P.A.

No further action

   G.S.

    15/7

To H.Q.
142 Inf Bde

Reference your Bx 22/100, Aug 5
Send you herewith my report as directed
by Adv: letter Gx 3/52

A Strathern
Lt Col. 1/20 London

Summs
24/6/17

To HQ
142 Inf Bde.

1. With reference to your Bd Letter G x 3/52 dated June 21st, the contents of the last paragraph of the letter have been communicated to the Officers concerned as directed by the Divisional Commander.

2. Reports by Captain English and 2/Lt Barker are attached as directed.

3. From Captain English's report it would appear that he issued no orders to withdraw until he did so at my direction; this would have been at about 12.30 noon after instructions had been received from the B.G.C. that a re-bombardment of the bag spit Bank would take place and that we must withdraw therefrom to allow of this re-bombardment.

   3/Lieuts Franshaw and Hitch report that the order to withdraw upon which they acted was a verbal order brought to them by a runner who stated that written orders to withdraw had been handed by him to 2/Lt Dean.

   2/Lt Franshaw says this message was received by him at about 10.45 a.m. and 2/Lt Hitch that it arrived between 11.30

and 11.45 am.

2/Lt Jackman states that he was close to 2/Lt Franshawe and Hitch but did not actually receive the message from this runner. He understood from Sergeant Parrott that the order to withdraw had been brought by this Sergeant, and as this N CO was exceptionally reliable and had come from Captain English he accepted and acted on the order. Captain English on the other hand says that he sent Sergt Parrott to reconnoitre and to bring back information only, and gave him no orders to deliver to any Officer.

4. I have made careful enquiries from all the Officers concerned and am of opinion that the message ordering withdrawal handed to 2/Lt Dean by a runner was, possibly from Capt Perkins to 2/Lt Dean (who belonged to Capt Perkins' Company) and was intended for him only. This opinion is based on the following facts:—

(a) The message was seen by 2/Lt Jackman in 2/Lt Dean's possession at about 11.30 am

3

written on an oblong buff slip. Capt.
Perkins had been using such slips
for his messages.

(c) 2/Lt Dean was apparently on the South
Side of the Canal at the time when he
received this message and his position
was critical.   2/Lt Barker says he
saw 2/Lt Dean retiring shortly before
he himself ordered his men to withdraw

5. I have made every effort to trace the runner
who took the message to 2/Lt Dean and
have personally interviewed all runners
still with the Battalion: both the runners
attached to 2/Lt Dean were killed. So far
the only trace I can find of a message
having been sent to 2/Lt Dean is from
a runner (Rifleman Sagar) who was
attached to Advanced Bn H.Q. on June 7th
He states that on the morning of that day
he saw another runner (Rifleman
Jackson) starting off with a message
and that as he passed him this runner
called to Rifleman Sagar that he was
taking a message to 2/Lt Dean. The
time is not certain but was
apparently before 10.15 a.m. This
Rifleman Jackson was in consequence of

badly wounded but I am trying to get into touch with him and with Sergeant Parrott with a view to tracing if possible the origin and contents of the message &c in question.

6. In view of all the circumstances above mentioned the contents of the last paragraph of the Divisional Commander's letter have been communicated to 2/Lts Franshaw, Kirk and Jackman.

Arthur Hutchins
Lt Col 1/7 of London

SERCUS
24/6/17

From O.C. 'C' Coy
    J.S.R.
To The Adjutant.
    J.S.R.   22-6-7.

With reference to Divisional letter G x 3/52
    Nos 9 and 11 Platoons went to W. end of SPOILBANK
to try and carry forward preceding waves.
    I left a party under Sgt COCKING on N side of
CANAL and took over the remainder in an endeavour
to get in touch with Battn on right.
    Immediately on crossing we were met with heavy
M.G. + rifle fire. Several casualties occurred.
    The party which actually went up the Southern
Bank was in the nature of a reconnoitring patrol
and consisted of myself and 9 men. 50% of these
became casualties before top of bank could be reached.
The remainder (of my original party) (about 12 to 15 men) were left under
what cover could be found lower down the bank.
    Having sent back for re-inforcements (my idea
being an attempt to rush the bank) I and my
party lay low for some 30 or 40 minutes and
it was not until heavy shrapnel began bursting
over us and the position was absolutely untenable
that I withdrew to the NORTHERN BANK where I commenced
digging in. I did not withdraw from here until
ordered to do so in view of the re-bombardment

Every effort was made to push forward but the accuracy and intensity of enemy's fire from M.G. on EASTERN end of SPOIL BANK and snipers on NORTHERN BANK made movement impossible.

The ground vacated was extremely heavy, consisting of mud and clay, and consolidation under condition of enemy's fire and nature of ground was impracticable.

      Y C Barker
        2nd Lieut
       O.C. "C" Coy
       1/21 London Reg.

SERCUS
22.6.17

To 1/21st London Regt.

Reference G.X. 3/52. 21st June. 1917.

I issued no orders whatever on my own responsibility to 2/Lt JACKMAN D Company to retire at 9.45. a.m. Z day.

I issued no orders whatever to any officer, N.C.O, or man, to retire, during the time that I was in command at Advanced Bn H.Q's (6.20.a.m to 10.15 a.m. Z day).

On the contrary, when the attack was held up, I did my utmost to push it with reinforcements, sending forward my reserve platoon (C.Coy), and applying for support both to my own Bn H.Q's (9.15 a.m) and to the 1/22nd L.R. who were on the spot. The latter placed 100 men at my disposal, at about the time I handed over to Lt Col HUTCHENCE (10.15.a.m)

At about 11.30.a.m. after Lt Col HUTCHENCE had been in communication with Brigade, I wrote out his order for all troops to withdraw from SPOIL BANK. I do not remember whether Lt Col HUTCHENCE or I signed it. It was sent by runner. 2/Lt HITCH, 2/Lt FRANSHAM, and 2/Lt JACKMAN, the three officers who were with the troops on the SPOIL BANK, reported at Advanced Bn H.Q. between 12 noon and 12.30 pm.

Sercus
June 22/1917

Englashnglish Capt
1/21st London Regt

H.Q.
142 Inf Bde

Reference your No. 43 of the 10th instant, I
beg to submit herewith a report of the
operations carried out by the unit under
my command on the 7th instant. Reports
by envisaging platoon Commanders are
enclosed.

Arthur Whitelaw
Major O/C London

Field
13/6/17

OPERATION ORDER 150   COPY No. 1
                       7-6-17

1/20th LONDON REGT. will attack the enemy position from O.5.B.7.7 to O.5.B.1.5. thence southwards along OBLIQUE ROW O.5.D.2.8. thence westward to O.5.C.8.7. where they will join up with 23rd LONDON REGT.

C. Coy will attack on the left, A Coy in the CENTRE & D Coy south of the Canal on the right.

Prior to the attack the whole of the objectives will be bombarded with heavy artillery. This bombardment will cease at 6.55 P.M. A creeping barrage will be placed in front of the position of assembly at 6.55 P.M. It will move at the rate of 100 yards per 5 minutes & lift off the position to be assaulted at 7 P.M. at which time the objectives will be assaulted.

POSITION OF ASSEMBLY
C & A Coys will assemble between the points O.5.A.5.7. and O.5.A.5.4.

D Coy. will assemble between the points O.5.A.5.1. and O.5.A.6.6. and will attack and consolidate their objective.

O.C. "D" Coy will establish an advanced strong post at the junction of OBLIQUE ROW and OPTIC TRENCH O.5.D.3.6. Companies will attack on a two Platoon frontage in 2 waves. A strong point will be established on the left flank of the captured objective.

O.C. "C" Coy will establish advanced H.Qs. in the QUARRY at O.5.A.4.9. and be in charge of operations during which he will keep in touch with O.C. 21st LONDON REGT. who will render him any assistance as the occasion arise.

R. E. Pewett
2/Lt & A/Adjt.
1/20th Bn London Regt.

Message

..........DIVISION.
Map reference
or Mark on Map
at back.

1. My {Company / Platoon} has reached..............
2. My {Company / Platoon} is at............ and is consolidating.
3. My {Company / Platoon} is at............and, has consolidated.
4. Am held up by M.G. at..............
5. I need :— Ammunition.
   Bombs.
   Rifle Grenades.
   Water.
   Very lights.
   Stokes shells.
6. Counter attack forming up at.............
7. I am in touch with..............on {Right / Left} at...........
8. I am not in touch with................on {Right / Left}
9. I am being shelled from..............
10. I estimate my present strength at............rifles.
11. Hostile {Battery / Machine Gun / Trench Mortar} active at..............

Time.......... m.   Name..............
Date............   Platoon..............
                       Company..............
                       Battalion..............

Arrived at A line at 5.0 AM.
Left A line at 5.35 AM
Arrived B line at 6.15 AM
Left B line till 6.55 AM
Arrived C line at 7-15 AM

Message

.....DIVISION.
Map reference
or Mark on Map
at back.

1. My {Company} has reached...........
   {Platoon }
2. My {Company} is at............ and is consolidating.
   {Platoon }
3. My {Company} is at............and has consolidated.
   {Platoon }
4. Am held up by M.G. at................
5. I need :—Ammunition.
            Bombs.
            Rifle Grenades.
            Water.
            Very lights.
            Stokes shells.
6. Counter attack forming up at.............
7. I am in touch with..............on Right at...........
                                    Left
8. I am not in touch with.............on Right
                                        Left
9. I am being shelled from..............
10. I estimate my present strength at............rifles.
11. Hostile {Battery   } active at.................
            {Machine Gun   }
            {Trench Mortar }

Time.......... m.   Name...............
Date.............   Platoon............
                     Company............
                     Battalion..........

Message

..........DIVISION.
Map reference
or Mark on Map
at back.

1. My {Company} has reached..........
      {Platoon}

2. My {Company} is at.......... and is consolidating.
      {Platoon}

3. My {Company} is at.......... and has consolidated.
      {Platoon}

4. Am held up by M.G. at..........

5. I need:— Ammunition.
            Bombs.
            Rifle Grenades.
            Water.
            Very lights.
            Stokes shells.

6. Counter attack forming up at..........

7. I am in touch with..........on Right at..........
                                  Left

8. I am not in touch with..........on Right
                                      Left

9. I am being shelled from..........

10. I estimate my present strength at..........rifles.

11. Hostile {Battery
             Machine Gun   active at..........
             Trench Mortar}

Time..........m.   Name..........
Date..........   Platoon..........
                    Company..........
                    Battalion..........

12 Platoon (M Coy) 4/1 "J 3"

..........DIVISION.
Map reference
or Mark on Map
at back.

Message

1. My {Company / Platoon} has reached..........
2. My {Company / Platoon} is at............ and is consolidating.
3. My {Company / Platoon} is at............ and has consolidated.
4. Am held up by M.G. at..............
5. I need:—Ammunition.
   Bombs.
   Rifle Grenades.
   Water.
   Very lights.
   Stokes shells.
6. Counter attack forming up at..........
7. I am in touch with............on {Right / Left} at..........
8. I am not in touch with............ on {Right / Left}
9. I am being shelled from............
10. I estimate my present strength at............rifles.
11. Hostile {Battery / Machine Gun / Trench Mortar} active at............

Time.........m.   Name..............
Date...........   Platoon............
                  Company............
                  Battalion...........

ZYX = Development & route taken ff platoon
X = Point where held up
Y = Jumped off to attack Spoil Bank

Message

..........DIVISION.
Map reference
or Mark on Map
at back.

1. My {Company / Platoon} has reached..................
2. My {Company / Platoon} is at............ and is consolidating.
3. My {Company / Platoon} is at............ and has consolidated.
4. Am held up by M.G. at..................
5. I need:—Ammunition.
    Bombs.
    Rifle Grenades.
    Water.
    Very lights.
    Stokes shells.
6. Counter attack forming up at..................
7. I am in touch with............ on Right at............
                              on Left at............
8. I am not in touch with............ on Right
                                    on Left
9. I am being shelled from..................
10. I estimate my present strength at............ rifles.
11. Hostile {Battery / Machine Gun / Trench Mortar} active at............

Time.......... m.   Name..................
Date..............   Platoon..................
                     Company..................
                     Battalion..................

13 Platoon
A Walsh
Sgt

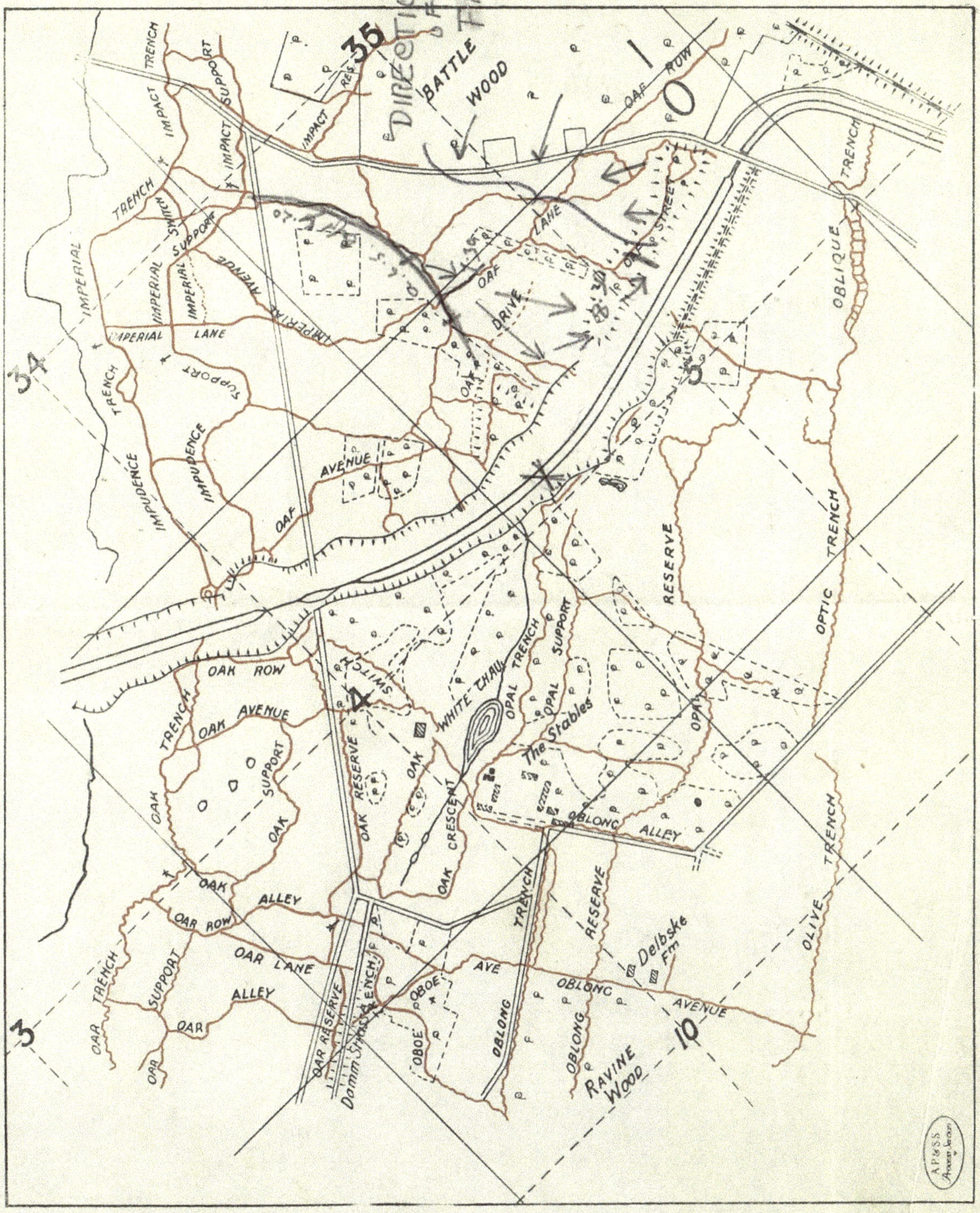

PRINTED BY No 2 ADVANCED SECTION. A P & S.S.

D Coy.

.... DIVISION

Map reference or Mark on MAP on Back.

1. I am at..........
2. I am at.......... and am consolidating
3. I am at.......... and have consolidated
4. Am held up by M.G. at..........
5. I need :- Ammunition
   Bombs
   Rifle Grenades
   Water
   Very Lights
   Stokes shells
6. Counter-attack forming up at..........
7. I am in touch with.......... on RIGHT at..........
   on LEFT at..........
8. I am not in touch on RIGHT..........
   LEFT..........
9. Am being shelled from..........
10. I estimate my present strength at.......... rifles
11. Hostile {BATTERY, MACHINE GUN, TRENCH MORTAR} active at..........

Time..........m Name..........
Date.......... Platoon..........
Company..........
Battalion..........

Message

..........DIVISION.
Map reference
or Mark on Map
at back.

1. My (Company) has reached..................
   (Platoon)
2. My (Company) is at............ and is consolidating.
   (Platoon)
3. My (Company) is at............ and has consolidated.
   (Platoon)
4. Am held up by M.G. at..................
5. I need :—Ammunition.
            Bombs.
            Rifle Grenades.
            Water.
            Very lights.
            Stokes shells.
6. Counter attack forming up at..................
7. I am in touch with.............. on Right at..........
                                    Left   Right
8. I am not in touch with............ on Left
9. I am being shelled from..................
10. I estimate my present strength at..........rifles.
11. Hostile { Battery
             Machine Gun } active at..............
            { Trench Mortar }

Time.......... m.   Name..................
Date.............. Platoon..................
                    Company..................
                    Battalion..................

2⁴ Platoon "A" Coy

Message

................DIVISION.

Map reference or Mark on Map at back.

1. My {Company / Platoon} has reached................

2. My {Company / Platoon} is at................ and is consolidating.

3. My {Company / Platoon} is at................ and has consolidated.

4. Am held up by M.G. at................

5. I need :— Ammunition.
   Bombs.
   Rifle Grenades.
   Water.
   Very lights.
   Stokes shells.

6. Counter attack forming up at................

7. I am in touch with................ on {Right / Left} at................

8. I am not in touch with................ on {Right / Left}

9. I am being shelled from................

10. I estimate my present strength at................rifles.

11. Hostile {Battery / Machine Gun / Trench Mortar} active at................

Time............ m. Name................

Date................ Platoon................

Company................

Battalion................

Message

..........DIVISION.
Map reference
or Mark on Map
at back.

1. My {Company / Platoon} has reached..............
2. My {Company / Platoon} is at............. and is consolidating.
3. My {Company / Platoon} is at.............and has consolidated.
4. Am held up by M.G. at..............
5. I need:— Ammunition.
   Bombs.
   Rifle Grenades.
   Water.
   Very lights.
   Stokes shells.
6. Counter attack forming up at..............
7. I am in touch with..............on Right at..............
                                    Left
8. I am not in touch with..............on Right
                                        Left
9. I am being shelled from..............
10. I estimate my present strength at..............rifles.
11. Hostile {Battery / Machine Gun / Trench Mortar} active at..............

Time..........m.   Name..............
Date.............. Platoon..............
                    Company..............
                    Battalion..............

Army Form C. 2118.

1/2 London Regt
Vol 23

WAR DIARY
or
INTELLIGENCE SUMMARY.
(Erase heading not required.)

Instructions regarding War Diaries and Intelligence Summaries are contained in F. S. Regs., Part II. and the Staff Manual respectively. Title pages will be prepared in manuscript.

Place	Date	Hour	Summary of Events and Information	Remarks and references to Appendices
Refer MAPS 28.S.W. SHEET 28 LEFT SECTION RIGHT BDE FRONT. S of CANAL	JULY 1st		Battn in line. 2 companys up line. 2 in support. 1 in reserve. — Situation quiet work on Blue Line	
Refer Maps WYTSCHAETE/1000	JULY 2nd		Battn relieved by 1 company 10th Regt Warwick Regt. + 2 Companies 8th N. STAFFS REGT. — 22nd LONDON extended line to take over LEFT PLATOON FRONTAGE. Ref no O.11.2.2. On relief Battn proceeded to OLD FRENCH TRENCH B4 in SPOIL BANK	
	JULY 3rd to JULY 8th		Battn in OLD FRENCH TRENCH JESTAMINET LANE + vicinity of LOCK GATES. Hostile artillery active work Cable burying parties under 2nd Signal Coy. Parties under Canadian Tunnelling Company	
ONTARIO CAMP RENINGHELST	JULY 8/9th		Battn relieved by 6th LONDON REGT. proceeded to ONTARIO CAMP Nr RENINGHELST. TRAINING commenced 4 hrs per day. ROAD REPAIRING parties sent each day.	
Refer MAPS 28 NW 1/40.000 1st SECTION N of CANAL	JULY 15th		Battn relieved 19th LONDON REGT in LEFT SECTOR. Sector N of YPRES—COMINES CANAL	
	JULY 15th to 25		Battn in line. 3 Companies in front line. 1 company in reserve. July 18th Revd B. Plumptre killed. 2 offrs wounded at Alix H.Q. Hostile artillery very active. Plateau occupying outpost position + communication impossible by day. Enemy front line near mustard gas. 16 casualties from effects	
RIDGEWOOD CAMP	JULY 26th		Battn relieved by 22nd LONDON REGT. moved to RIDGEWOOD CAMP. 2 companies in dugouts behind RIDGEWOOD.	
MICKSKEN NEAR WESTOUTRE	JULY 26th 8p.m. to JULY 31st		Battn relieved by 22nd MIDDLESEX REGT. moved to MICKSKEN CAMP M.3.C.1.7). Battn under canvas at MICKSKEN. TRAINING 3½ hours per day	

[Signature] Lt. Col.
Commanding
1/21st LONDON REGT

WAR DIARY or INTELLIGENCE SUMMARY.

1/21st LONDON REGT. T.F.

WAR DIARY
INTELLIGENCE SUMMARY

Army Form C. 2118.

Vol 25

HAZEBROUCK 57A 1/100,000
BELGIUM 28 NW. 1/40,000
FRANCE 51.B NW. 1/20,000 Summary of Events and Information
LENS 11 1/100,000
BELGIUM & FRANCE 27 1/40,000

Place	Date	Hour	Summary of Events and Information	Remarks and references to Appendices
MENIN ROAD	1/2	2 a.m.	Battalion relieved in sector astride YPRES-MENIN ROAD by 9th Bn. Manchester Regt. after four days' tour during which heavy casualties were incurred by shell fire & on relief proceeded to CAVALRY BARRACKS, YPRES. 5 other ranks wounded during tour.	
YPRES	2	6 p.m.	Batt. relieved by 9th LOYAL N.LANCS Regt. & on relief proceeded to DOMINION LINES H.23.6.	
DOMINION LINES H.23.6.	5	9 a.m.	Batt. marched to STEENVOORDE AREA - remaining 5 days - during which time general training was carried out. Major Heslop went to Hospital sick & East Riff Tolleton (23rd London Regt) assumed command of Battalion.	
STEENVOORDE	10	8 a.m.	Batt. proceeded by 'buses to CHATEAU SEGARD area for a period of 6 days, during which time working parties were supplied in forward area. A draft of 2 officers & 30 other ranks joined the Battalion. Three of whom were wounded same day of joining.	
CH. SEGARD. H.30.Central				
WIPPENHOEK L.30c	16	8 a.m.	Battalion marched to DALLINGTON CAMP - WIPPENHOEK area to refit.	
EECKE P.17	18	8 a.m.	EECKE area, remaining 4 days for rest. Draft of 130 other ranks joined unit.	
	22/23	11 p.m.	BAVINGHOVE - entraining 1 a.m. for MARGEUIL - 1st Army area (XIII Corps)	
ST. AUBIN			arriving at 10 a.m. and marched to ST. AUBIN (LENS 11)	
	24	7.30 a.m.	Battalion proceeded by Light Railway from ST. CATHERINE detraining at WORCESTER SIDING and relieved 4th Bn. Bedfordshire Regt. in support. Working parties provided for forward area.	
RED LINE	26th	10.15 p.m.	Casualties caused to Working party by enemy Rifle Grenade wounding 2 officers & 3 other ranks and killing one other rank. 1 officer and two other ranks, namely 2nd Lt. Roberts died of wounds. 2nd Lt. Squibb and 2nd Lt. Roberts O.H.S., wounded. 2nd Lt. Roberts subsequently died of wounds.	
do	28th		Major Capt. R. Heslop returned from Hospital and assumed command of Battalion.	
do	24th to 30th		Working parties in forward area.	

3/10/17.

C.D.R. Heslop.
MAJOR.
COMMANDING
21st Bn. LONDON REGT.

WAR DIARY
or
INTELLIGENCE SUMMARY.

(Erase heading not required.)

Army Form C. 2118.

2/13 London Regt
October 1917
Vol 26

Place	Date	Hour	Summary of Events and Information	Remarks and references to Appendices
RED LINE	1st.		Battn in Support in RED LINE - OPPY Sector.	
OPPY	2nd -10th.		Battn holding Left Sector, Left Brigade Front - OPPY WOOD.	
	10th.		Battn relieved by 8th Lon: Regt. Proceeded in relief into reserve billets	
			at MAROEUIL. Armed Guard provided on arrival at MAROEUIL to control	
MAROEUIL			disturbance in Chinese Labour Camp.	
MAROEUIL	10th. -17th.		Battn in Reserve Billets at MAROEUIL. Refitting & training. Musketry training	
			on range at PONT DE PIERRE. Cable burying parties & pipe laying parties	
			provided in forward area. Daily guard furnished at Chinese Labour Camp.	
			MAROEUIL.	
	13th.		Major G. DAWES M.C. 2nd South Staffs assumed Command of the Battalion -	
	18th.		Battn moved into reserve Rifle Brigade hutments at ROUNDHAY CAMP.	
ROUNDHAY CAMP	18th-25th.		Battn in Brigade Reserve. Daily working parties on RED LINE, salvage,	
			& on road improvements.	
	19th.		A party of 10 o.r. with Officer proceeded forward in Tank Post &	
			assumed duties of 24th Lon: Regt. in NAVAL TRENCH.	
	26th.		Battn relieved 2nd Lon: Regt. in Left Sector, Right Brigade Front - Tank Post.	

Lt Col
Commanding
1/21 London Regt

21 Batt. London Regt.

Maps: Lens 11 1/40,000
51/3NW 1/20,000
Oppy 1/10,000

October 1917

Army Form C. 2118.

WAR DIARY
or
INTELLIGENCE SUMMARY.
(Erase heading not required.)

Place	Date	Hour	Summary of Events and Information	Remarks and references to Appendices
Front Line	26th–31st		Batt in Front Line, holding Mill Post. Work carried out:—	
			Works Post Scheme.	
(West of Gavrelle sector)				

J Dunn Lt Col
Commanding
1/21st London Regt

21st Batt'n. The London Regt.
(First Surrey Rifles)

1/21 London Regt

Vol 27

WAR DIARY
or
INTELLIGENCE SUMMARY.
(Erase heading not required.)

Army Form C. 2118.

Instructions regarding War Diaries and Intelligence Summaries are contained in F.S. Regs., Part II and the Staff Manual respectively. Title pages will be prepared in manuscript.

Place	Date	Hour	Summary of Events and Information	Remarks and references to Appendices
R2 Sector Front Line	1/11/17		The Brigadier visited the Batt'n in the morning.	
do.	2/11/17		Lieut: PARVIN, American Army, left after 3 days' visit to the Batt'n.	
do.	4/11/17	8.30 a.m.	D Coy. went down to RED LINE to make way for raiding Coy. of 23rd: Batt'n in HARENC TRENCH	
		4.30 p.m.	23rd & 24th: Bns. raid trenches E. of GAVRELLE. Our Company withdrawn from front line during raid. Colours rockets sent up from MILL POST by many Bns. Successful raid. 15 Prisoners. 4 M.G. 2 TM. - many enemy killed. Raiders' casualties very slight. 23rd: Bn: Casualties = 10 killed, 4 wd.	
do.	5/11/17		Batt'n relieved by 6th bn London Regt. - move into Reserve at WAKEFIELD CAMP.	
WAKEFIELD CAMP	6/11/17		Batt'n bathed at ROCLINCOURT - Company training.	
do.	7/11/17		Lewis Gun & musketry training.	
do.	8/11/17		Assault training under Staff Sergt: Assoc: Football. Offrs v. Sergeants (Offrs 2-1).	
do.	9/11/17		Musketry M.G. firing on range in ROCLINCOURT valley.	
do.	10/11/17		Inspect. & train. Box respirators inspected by Div: Gas NCO.	
do.	11/11/17	10.45 a.m.	Church Parade in Div. Cinema.	
do.	12/11/17		R4 Sector Kenwick	

A6945 Wt.W14422.M1180 330000 12/16 D.D.&I. Forms/C/2118/14.

2nd Batt: The Londown Regt.
(Post Service Rifles)

Army Form C. 2118.

WAR DIARY
or
INTELLIGENCE SUMMARY.
(Erase heading not required.)

Instructions regarding War Diaries and Intelligence
Summaries are contained in F. S. Regs., Part II.
and the Staff Manual respectively. Title pages
will be prepared in manuscript.

Place	Date	Hour	Summary of Events and Information	Remarks and references to Appendices
WAKEFIELD CAMP	13/11/17		Batt: relieving the 19th Lon Regt in Rt. Sector, going into Oppy front line to conform with Corps winter post scheme.	
OPPY	14/11/17		Much work to open Communication between Posts, & to make accommodation for garrison.	
Do.	15/11/17		The Div: Commander visited the line in the morning. G.S.O.1 31st Div. came round reconnoitring the line.	
Do.	16/11/17		Corps Relief Scheme Drafted. 2/G.S.O.1 visited the Area.	
Do.	17/11/17		Officer of 11/16: E. YORKS Regt: reconnoitred Batt: area. Major Rh. Toerson, M.C. rejoins from leave. 1 O.R. killed in OPPY POST.	
Do.	18/11/17		Brigade Commander visited the Batt: in this morning.	
Do.	19/11/17		Batt: relieved by 11/16: E. YORKS, & moved back to WAKEFIELD CAMP.	
WAKEFIELD CAMP	20/11/17		Batts refitting.	
Do.	21/11/17		Batt: paraded 9.30 am. & moved to MONT ST. ELOY (WINNIPEG CAMP) forming 2nd. Div: in the rord late evening. Moved to 3rd: Army Area.	
MONT St. ELOY	22/11/17		Parade 9.15 am. & moved to BERNEVILLE.	
BERNEVILLE	23/11/17		Batt: in billets at BERNEVILLE.	
Do.	24/11/17		Parade 7.30 am. & moved to GOMIECOURT.	

2/5th Batt. Tyneside Rifles
(9th Surrey Rifles)

WAR DIARY
or
INTELLIGENCE SUMMARY.

Army Form C. 2118.

Place	Date	Hour	Summary of Events and Information	Remarks and references to Appendices
GOMIECOURT	25/11/17		Paraded 1.20 p.m. for march via BAPAUME to BARASTRE. Much delay en route owing to congestion of traffic in BAPAUME.	
BARASTRE	26/11/17		Proportion of Battn. under Major R.H. TOLERTON less 1 Bn. Reinforcement Battn. at MAILLY-MAILLET.	
			Battn. paraded at 1 pm. for march to BEAUMETZ-LES-CAMBRAI.	
BEAUMETZ-LES-CAMBRAI	27/11/17		Battn. in camp at BEAUMETZ.	
Do	28/11/17		Battn. moved at 9 p.m. into HINDENBURG SUPPORT LINE - K.16.B.D.	
HINDENBURG SUPPORT LINE	29/11/17		Battn. H.Q. Established in K.16.F. - S.A.A., bombs ill. fraction drawn.	
Do	30/11/17		Heavy counter attack launched by enemy against BOURLON - MOEUVRES at 7 a.m. Battn. stands to, ready for move. Works on the HINDENBURG SUPPORT LINE forbade it impossible in own defences. 2/Lt. STRAWSON Bomb. P. Iny. carry S.A.A. forward for M.G. Box.	

Headquarters,
142 Inf. Bde.

Hereunder War Diary for
December, 1917.

[signature]
Capt. & Adjt.
for LT COL
COMMANDING
1/21st LONDON REGT

21st Battn. The London Regt.
First Surrey Rifles

WAR DIARY
INTELLIGENCE SUMMARY.
(Erase heading not required.)

Army Form C. 2118.

Ref. Maps — LENS 11 1/100,000
FRANCE { Sheet 57c 1/40,000
ALBERT (Combined Sheet) 1/40,000
(MOEUVRES Special Sheet 1/20,000

Vol 28

Place	Date	Hour	Summary of Events and Information	Remarks and references to Appendices
HINDENBURG SUPPORT LINE	1/12/17	9.30 a.m.	Orders received to be ready to move at once to reinforce either 140 or 141 Inf. Bde.	
		3 p.m.	Supporting positions W. & E. of ANNEUX. Warning received of probable relief of 15th. Lon. Regt. in BOURLON WOOD.	
		5 p.m.	Orders received to reinforce 141 Inf. Bde. E. of ANNEUX. Battn. prepare to move.	
		6 p.m.	Orders cancelled & new orders received to proceed into the relief of 15th. London Regt. already prepared for.	
BOURLON WOOD	2/12/17	1 a.m.	Relief of 15th. Lon. Regt. complete. Dispositions — D & A Coys. in front line, opposite BOURLON — C Coy. in immediate support — B Coy. in reserve near Battn. Hqrs: at J.W. corner of BOURLON WOOD.	
		8.10 p.m.	7th. Bde. Lon. Regt. attack to straighten W. of BOURLON WOOD. Our L.G. cooperate on R. flank of this attack. Capt. A.L. SHEKLAND sent on platoon (D Coy.) to assist in the consolidation of captured line. 8th. Lon. Regt. to avoid & gunners wounded, passed through Battn. Hq. R.A.P.	
	3/12/17	1 a.m.	Stretcher-bearers & S.A.A. supplied to 8th. Bn. to help in evacuation of wounded & consolidation. C.O. issues orders for new dispositions to strengthen the left flank, after report of O.C. 8th. Bn.	
		1.45 a.m.	These orders cancelled on receipt of orders from 142 Inf. Bde. to take over our front line on the Right Flank, in relief of a company of 22nd. Bn.	
			Heavy enemy shelling — GAS — H.E. — around Battn. Hq. in the evening. Platoons relieved by cubical during Trafford fire.	
	4/12/17	3 p.m.	Orders received from Brigade for C.O. to go to Bn. Hqrs. He returns at 5.30 p.m. with orders for withdrawal of Battn. Hqrs:	
Do.		6 p.m.	From BOURLON SALIENT. Operation Orders issued to O.C. Coys. in conference at Battn. Hqrs:	

21st. Batt. The London Regt:
First Surrey Rifles

WAR DIARY
INTELLIGENCE SUMMARY
(Erase heading not required.)

Army Form C. 2118.

December, 1917.

Instructions regarding War Diaries and Intelligence Summaries are contained in F. S. Regs., Part II. and the Staff Manual respectively. Title pages will be prepared in manuscript.

Place	Date	Hour	Summary of Events and Information	Remarks and references to Appendices
BOURLON WOOD	4/12/17	4-10 p.m.	Vicinity of Battn. Hqrs: intermittently heavily bombarded with GAS shell & H.E. S.A.A. stocks removed by limbers about 9 p.m.	
Do.	4/5 12/17	12 midnight	Battn. withdraws according to plan to HINDENBURG SUPPORT LINE - Casualties, Lieut: HUNT killed. 2 O.R. wounded.	
	5/12/17	4 a.m.	Outpost Line (2 platoons, C Coy.) under Lieut. J. EDMUNDS withdrew without casualty from BOURLON WOOD.	4A
HINDENBURG SUPPORT	Do.	6.30 a.m.	Outpost line reports lost with the Battn.	
			Battn. extended in accordance with 142 Inf. Bde: O.O. 240. Disposition - 4 Companies took up forward in depth, 2 platoons in main line of resistance, 1 platoon in outpost line. Major R.H. TOLERTON came forward to relieve Lt.Col. DAWES - temporarily assumed command of Battn. Battn. Hq: in 5.9" gun pits in forward trench system.	4B
Do.	6/12/17	11 a.m.	Divisional Commander visited the line.	
		4 p.m.	Fighting patrol under W/S. J.O.B. HITCH sent Northward along HINDENBURG SUPPORT LINE obtains touch with outposts of 2nd. Batt: Devon: - no signs of enemy patrols.	
		5.30 p.m.	Thin forward outpost line through GRAINCOURT held by 140 Inf. Bde: with Drawn.	
		6 p.m.	Post in K.11.a. (Sheet 57c), held by Reinf: relieved by 2 platoons, D Coy., under Lieut: C.R. EDMUNDS.	4B
			Patrols & forward picquets maintained during this & succeeding nights.	
Do.	7/12/17		Work of consolidation & wiring continued. Enemy M.G. & snipers active from GRAINCOURT & neigh[bour]hood.	
			Much desultory shelling around Battn. Hqrs. Patrols &c. maintained.	

21st: Batn. Frederick Ref:
'21st Surrey Rifles'

Army Form C. 2118.

WAR DIARY
INTELLIGENCE SUMMARY.
(Erase heading not required.)

Instructions regarding War Diaries and Intelligence Summaries are contained in F.S. Regs., Part II. and the Staff Manual respectively. Title pages will be prepared in manuscript.

Place	Date	Hour	Summary of Events and Information	Remarks and references to Appendices
HINDENBURG SUPPORT LINE.	7/12/17	9 p.m.	Batn. Hqrs. moved from forward system into GEORGE STR., near Bn. Hqrs. An advanced Hqrs. in left Batn. Hqrs.	
do.	8/12/17		in the old position, under Capt. SMERLANO. Lieut. Col. DAWES resumed command of the Batn. Work of consolidation improvement of wire and communication continued. Day quieter and enemy in general less active.	A9
do.	9/12/17		Considerable hostile shelling against our posts resulting in the evacuation of a post on our right garrisoned by the 22nd Battalion London Regt. A counter attack consisting of 20 O.R.'s with a Platoon in support was commanded by 2nd Lt. STONE. This operation resulted in driving the enemy back to exit of the Sunken road in K.18.c. but further progress was impossible owing to heavy machine gun fire down the road. Lt. Pickard and 2 O.R.'s killed. Sgt ALEXANDER whilst he was shot through the thigh early in the morning, stripped away from the regiment and got entrenched to the left. When the enemy were attacking, he left the trench and charged and disposed of a party of the enemy with the bayonet but was killed while performing this act of gallantry. Advance Patrol under Lt. H. EDMUNDS established.	A9
do.	9-10 12/17	12 midnight		

2/8. Batt. The London Regt
"J. Victoria Rifles"

Army Form C. 2118.

December 1917

WAR DIARY
of
INTELLIGENCE SUMMARY.

(Erase heading not required.)

Instructions regarding War Diaries and Intelligence Summaries are contained in F. S. Regs., Part II. and the Staff Manual respectively. Title pages will be prepared in manuscript.

Place	Date	Hour	Summary of Events and Information	Remarks and references to Appendices
HINDENBURG SUPPORT LINE	10/12/17		Day exceedingly quieter. Attack by 11.A GILKES M.G. and BORI went out to the old advanced post at K.11.A. concealed previous night. A number of P bombs were thrown into the dugouts and the entrance to the tunnels.	
do	11/12/17		Consolidation continued. Situation fairly quiet except for some shelling from GRAINCOURT	
do	12/12/17		do	
do	do	6pm	Two Conferences returned by 23rd Bn Royal Fusiliers. Remaining Companies relieved about midnight by the 22 Bn The London Regiment.	
K 32 a + c	13/12/17	2am	Relief complete. Battalion bivouacked to the side.	
do	14/12/17		Area reached cleaned up generally. Blankets put up and all efforts made to make things as comfortable as possible.	
do	15/12/17	6pm	Reserve to the 7th Bn The London Regt.	
BERTINCOURT	do	9pm	Battalion in billets at BERTINCOURT.	
do	16/12/17	8am	Battalion paraded and marched to VELU. Entrained there at 9am and proceeded to AVELUY. Detraining there about midday. Bivouac in huts and from then marched to LAVIEVILLE which was reached 4.30pm	
LAVIEVILLE	17/12/17		Day spent cleaning up generally and return economy	

21st Battn. The London Regt.
First Surrey Rifles.

WAR DIARY
INTELLIGENCE SUMMARY.
(Erase heading not required.)

December, 1917.

Army Form C. 2118.

Place	Date	Hour	Summary of Events and Information	Remarks and references to Appendices
LUNEVILLE	17/12/17 to 30/12/17		Battalion in billets resting. Light training carried out according to daily programme. Tactical schemes by Brigade under supervision of the Divisional Commander. Work done, as material available, on temporary accommodation in billets. Christmas Holiday.	
	28/12/17		Brigade put under orders to move at 4 hours' notice.	
	29/12/17	4 pm.	Orders received to be ready to move about 6 pm.	
	30/12/17	6.15 pm.	Brigade Operation Order received to march to ALBERT train for ETRICOURT.	
		9 pm.	Battalion entrained at ALBERT.	
ETRICOURT	31/12/17	6.30 am.	Battalion under canvas in Camp near ETRICOURT.	
	31/12/17 to 1/1/18 12 midnight		Operation Order received from Brigade to move into Camp in LECHELLE area, 1/1/18.	

G.D. Warkinton. T.M.
1/21 London Regt.

2nd Bat: The London Regt:
First Surrey Rifles

Army Form C. 2118.

Ref: Maps:- FRANCE, Sheet 57c. 1/40,000.
HOEUVRES, Sheet 57c. 1/20,000.

WAR DIARY
or
INTELLIGENCE SUMMARY.
(Erase heading not required.)

Place	Date	Hour	Summary of Events and Information	Remarks and references to Appendices
ETRICOURT	1/1/18		The Battn. left Camp at ETRICOURT & marched to huts at LECHELLE. The Commanding Officer rode out to reconnoitre ground held by 1/C Bn. (R.N.) Divn. in the neighbourhood of VILLERS PLOUICH.	
LECHELLE	2/1/18		In Camp at LECHELLE.	
Do.	3/1/18		The Battn. moved into huts Adjugnods (HAWKES CAMP) in HAVRINCOURT WOOD. Major R.H.TOLERTON. M.C. left for England to attend Senior Officers' Course at ALDERSHOT.	
HAVRINCOURT WOOD	4/1/18		A reconnoitring party went into the trenches to make arrangements to take relief of 1st 9th R.W.F. (19th Div.) at RIBECOURT. Later during the Battn. marched to RIBECOURT & relieved the 9th R.W.F. in the line. Dispositions- B & C Coys in Front line, D in Support Hdqrs. at the BRASSERIE RIBECOURT. A Coy was attached to act as Counterattack Company for the 24th Battn. into who held the PREMY Salient on our immediate Right.	
Front Line RIBECOURT	5/1/18		Continued tour. Battn. in the line.	
Do.	6/1/18		The Divisional Commander & Brigadier visited the line. First thaw after weeks of frost & rain.	
Do.	7/1/18		The Corps Commander visited Battn. Hqrs: A Coy. relieved B Coy. in the Right Front line. Remained from	
Do.	8/1/18		Heavy snow showers.	
Do.	9/1/18		Snow fell during the afternoon & evening. A Coy. relieved C Coy. in L.C. Left Front line. Enemy attacked our counter attack Coy. to 24th Battn.	

21st. Batn. The London Regt.
First Surrey Rifles.

Army Form C. 2118.

WAR DIARY
INTELLIGENCE SUMMARY.
(Erase heading not required.)

January, 1918.

Ref. Maps:-
FRANCE Sheet 57c 1/40,000
MOEUVRES Special Sheet 1/20,000

Place	Date	Hour	Summary of Events and Information	Remarks and references to Appendices
FRONT LINE RIBECOURT	10/1/18		A heavy thaw set in. The melting of snow and rain in the trenches and becoming into them of melted its snow from the trenches made the sides of trenches difficult of passage; in many places water collected to depth of 3 feet. There was a marked increase in enemy artillery activity.	
DO	11/1/18		The whole Corps Artillery carried out protection shoot at dawn.	
DO	14/1/18		The Batn. was relieved by the 6th. Bn. Batn. & proceeded by road to TRESCAULT – thence by light railway to YTRES to Camp at LECHELLE.	
LECHELLE.	15/1/18 – 17/1/18		The Batn. in camp at LECHELLE. Baths rationing Economy & Company training as opportunity afford. The weather was generally warmer than the roads & country very not roundly.	
DO.	17/1/18		Reconnoitering parts went to FLESQUIERES. The Brigade part of the Batn. attended a performance by 63rd (R.N.) Divl. Follies at LECHELLE.	
DO	18/1/18		The Batn. relieved the 9th. Batn. & 1 Company 18th. Battn. in the Left Front line, FLESQUIERES Sector, march & light railway from YTRES to TRESCAULT. The enemy was raising a par.	
			19th. Divn. front during the arrival of our company + a heavy gun shell bursts were exploded by 8.15 p.m. Relief proceeded along the GRAND RAVINE without casualty.	
			Dispositions – C & B front line + D in support. Battn. Hqrs. in HINDENBURG SUPPORT LINE.	

T. Damned Henmyway

1st. Batn. The London Regt:
First Surrey Rifles.

January, 1918.

Ref: Maps:-
FRANCE Sheet 57c. 1/40,000
MOEUVRES Special Sheet 1/20,000.

Army Form C. 2118.

WAR DIARY
INTELLIGENCE SUMMARY.
(Erase heading not required.)

Instructions regarding War Diaries and Intelligence Summaries are contained in F. S. Regs., Part II. and the Staff Manual respectively. Title pages will be prepared in manuscript.

Place	Date	Hour	Summary of Events and Information	Remarks and references to Appendices
FLESQUIERES	19/1/18		A quiet day. One unlucky shell destroyed our left L.G. post — 1 man killed, 3 wounded.	
Do.	20/1/18		Slight enemy shelling of battery area. 2/Lt: L. SWEETING slightly wounded while on patrol.	
Do.	21/1/18		Intn.-Company reliefs at dusk.	
Do.	22/1/18		The Corps Commander visited Batn's Hqrs:	
Do.	24/1/18		The Batn. was relieved at nightfall by 22/R: Batn: Troops drew into support in HINDENBURG SUPPORT LINE	
Do.	19/1/18 –24/1/18		During this period the front line efforts were mainly concentrated upon work in the line itself. A number of T. Heads were Dug according to Divisional Orders for the accommodation of the garrison of the posts. Repeated patrols went out to investigate the Gun pits & half tramways K.12.D. in which the enemy had established a stray post; patrols it was hoped to raid. 2/Lt: Pte HUMPHREYS was congratulated by the Divisional Commander on one such patrol.	
Do.	25/1/18		The Batn: in support. Attachment practised evacuation by Day & night. Enemy aeroplanes dropped bombs in BERTINCOURT during the night. Damaging hired vehicles at the Transport Lines but causing no casualty.	
Do.	26/1/18 27/1/18		Attack with practised at strawdum by Day & night. On 27th: Lt: Col: G. DAWES, D.S.O., M.C. left from tour of 6 months' duty at home. Major T.O. BURY, R.W.F., a/o 1/24 K: London Regt: assumed Command.	

Ruwart Demarai Memorymaja

2nd Batt: The London Regt.
First Surrey Rifles

WAR DIARY
or
INTELLIGENCE SUMMARY.
(Erase heading not required.)

Army Form C. 2118.

January, 1918.

Ref. Maps:
FRANCE - Sheet 57c. 1/40,000.
NEUVIRES - Special Sheet 1/20,000.

Instructions regarding War Diaries and Intelligence Summaries are contained in F. S. Regs., Part II. and the Staff Manual respectively. Title pages will be prepared in manuscript.

Place	Date	Hour	Summary of Events and Information	Remarks and references to Appendices
FRESNOIRES	28/1/18		Battn relieved by 23rd Lon Regt: (less 2 Companies) & proceeded by march & light railway to YPRES, thence to Camps. A & D Coys. at LITTLE WOOD CAMP, YPRES, B & C Coys. at LECHELLE. Batt: joined 140th Inf Bde:	
YPRES	29/1/18		Enemy aeroplanes over lines areas at night.	
	30/1/18		Protracted raid by enemy aeroplanes during the night 30th/31st. Many bombs and troops in the vicinity of YPRES.	
to	31/1/18		The Battn moved to huts & tents in BERTINCOURT. A working party of 200 men with officers NCOs in proportion worked on the defensive line near TRESCAULT. The Army Commander visited the Essex Trench.	
			A draft of 4 Offs: 145 or. from the Disbands 2/11th London Regt. joined the Battn in the evening.	

30 January, 1918.

T. Osmond Hunt Major
Commanding 1/21st London Regt.